Artful Collage
FROM
Found Objects

Artful Collage
FROM
Found Objects

ELLEN SPECTOR PLATT

STACKPOLE
BOOKS

For Mark Hopkins

Copyright ©2012 by Ellen Spector Platt

Published by
STACKPOLE BOOKS
5067 Ritter Road
Mechanicsburg, PA 17055
www.stackpolebooks.com

Printed in the United States of America

10 9 8 7 6 5 4 3 2 1

FIRST EDITION

Cover design by Caroline Stover

Library of Congress Cataloging-in-Publication Data

Platt, Ellen Spector.
    Artful collage from found objects / Ellen Spector Platt. -- FIRST EDITION.
        pages   cm
        ISBN 978-0-8117-0119-8 (pbk.)
        1. Collage—Technique. I. Title.
TT910.P55 2012
751.4'93—dc23

2012004051

Contents

Acknowledgments

For this book, more than the others I've written, appreciation must be expressed. First, I thank Kyle Weaver, my editor for five books at Stackpole, for his confidence that I could shift to a new medium and for his humor, openness, and skill—everything one could hope for in an editor.

Artist Jerilyn Jurinek was my first collage instructor. Everyone should be so lucky to experience such a talented teacher, one who can restrict choices and expand them at the same time. Jerilyn is one of those special teachers who can change how you view the world.

Several other artists allowed me to present their work here, all of them fairly new to collage. I'm delighted with their various points of view: Judith Benson, Jen Hopkins, and Judith Wolfson. Each is identified with her work throughout these pages.

Friends and family overwhelmed me with offers of stuff to be used in my designs; their friends and family did as well, unto the third generation. Some went out on streets and town dumps to find items that they knew I could use. Others just emptied their drawers. Sarah Hopkins, Jen Hopkins, Ellen Luger, Linda Platt, Ben Platt, Lucy Platt, Annabelle Platt, Joan Steel, Betsy Williams, and Ellen Zachos found great stuff. A special thank you to Mark Hopkins, who is always ready to aid and abet, for offering goodies from his stash of old stuff and his talents as a wood artist. Fran Burton and Ellie Weinstein allowed me the privilege of using their apartments for photography.

My collage group—Liz Curtin, Kathleen O'Reilly, Linda Perry-Lube, Aileen Robrish, and Lauren Blankstein—contributed wonderful supplies, invaluable design suggestions, critiques, and enthusiasm.

For those who were embarrassed to be walking around the city with me when I stopped to pick up the perfect collage element from the curb or a trash can, I offer my apologies.

Basics

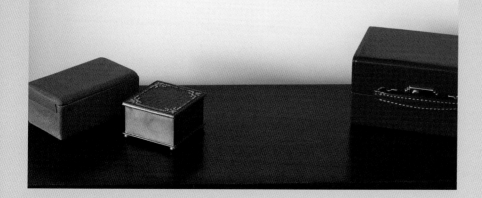

You can create collage artwork from junk and treasured objects, stuff you find around the house, leftovers from craft projects started and discarded long ago, keepsakes you've tucked away, bits and pieces in the backs of drawers, and papers torn from old magazines and newsprint.

Use collage techniques to design a piece of wall art that you can enjoy at home or in the office, or give away as gift to be long cherished.

Some collage is like scrapbooking, where you design each page to tell a story. The collages in this book might tell a story, complete within their own boundaries, but many of the designs are abstract; torn and cut papers and other materials are assembled in new and interesting ways and presented within mat and frame, or informally, without mat and frame.

You will experience particular pleasure from dragging out old stuff at home and scouring the environment wherever you find yourself. Might that gold foil wrapper of the chocolate bar you just devoured form the perfect sun for your next summer sky? Would those tongue depressors I spy shivering in the examining room be just the thing I need to make a small frame? And why did I keep the old license plate from the Jeep I drove on my farm ten years ago, if not to form the centerpiece of my latest 3-D collage featuring rusty metal objects?

My fat French dictionary says that "collage" means pasting or gluing, but sometimes glue isn't the best way to adhere heavy or irregular items. You'll wind up pinning, tacking, nailing, or tying elements to your artwork. It may feel more like sculpture. Who cares!

You will see how to manipulate the stuff that you gather for collage—bending, cutting, tearing, folding, fringing, rolling, stretching, felting, crumpling, creasing, flattening, ironing, hammering, pleating, coiling, spiraling, painting, dyeing, sewing, and tying.

Rely on your sense of humor, your visual and tactile perceptions, your emotions, and your thoughts to have a wonderful time.

What You Need

For each of the forty-six projects in this book, I list the materials I used. I don't expect you to replicate the projects, but only to have a good idea of what I did and how I did it, so that you can adapt the projects or use them as a stimulus for your own work.

Some of the supplies, like glue, scissors, brushes, pencils, and rulers, will become part of your permanent collage kit. Materials, such as particular papers, objects, and pictures, are specific to one design.

Paper

Traditionally, collage is about gluing cut or torn papers to make an artwork. Because in this book I stress recycled, reused, and repurposed materials, I find most of the colorful papers in magazines and newspapers, ads and inserts, old calendars, catalogues, brochures, gift wrap, tissue paper, foil wrappers, greeting cards and envelopes, maps, train schedules, used concert and event tickets, sheet music, composition paper, labels, family photos, playing cards, canceled stamps on envelopes, and construction paper in colors that the children reject.

I cut out and save stuff in file folders by color tone and also by topic. I've had in mind a collage theme of watches and clocks, and filed away many glossy ads and pictures for about six months (see the results on p. 120).

Of course there are many exquisite handmade and machine-made art papers offered for sale, and the temptation is to run to a fine art store and buy. But I resist. I also resist stickers and lettering found in scrapbooking departments of craft stores. I'd rather draw, make, or cut out what I need from free sources.

For the forty-six collages in this book, I've bought only eight sheets of art paper, a pack of colored tissue, and a pad of watercolor paper to make my own painted papers. The rest is found and saved.

Hand-Painted or Printed Paper

With a pad of watercolor paper and a small set of watercolor or acrylic paints, or both, you can make your own papers to later cut or tear and incorporate into a collage. I worked with my two favorite girls, my granddaughters, ages eight and ten, to make the papers shown here. We brushed on acrylic paints, then for some, we used fingers, a comb, or the end of a paintbrush to make marks and texture. In one project, I cut our hand-painted and hand-printed papers to form an abstract collage.

Glue, Paste, and Other Useful Adhesives

You will not be happy if your collage falls apart when you go to hang it at home, or even more embarrassing, when you present it as a gift. You need a strong attachment, but once paper or another element has been glued down, it can't be removed without leaving a gaping hole or other unsightly roughage on the surface of your board. If you've made a mistake, it's usually better to cover it up by gluing something else on top, painting over it, or living with it than trying to rip it out. So plan ahead. Chef Julia Child was an expert in showing how to correct errors in cooked food or baking by sprinkling on additional herbs or dolloping on the frosting, and her principles might be applied to collage as well.

It makes perfect sense to think that lighter elements, such as paper, use lighter glues. When you're using heavier elements in your collage, like the license plate on p. 39, you'll need a strong adhesive. Below is a list of the adhesives I used in the projects, but many are interchangeable. You certainly don't need all of those listed below, but it's nice to know there are options when trying to attach recalcitrant materials.

Smooth paper after each pasting with a plastic credit card or a roller to force out air bubbles, or you can let paper wrinkle for texture. Remember though that if the bottom layer is wrinkled, all the papers on top will also look wrinkled.

- **White Glue.** Elmer's is a reliable brand. Use this for heavier papers. Brush on the entire surface at full strength. Also brush on the section of the board you are covering. After positioning your paper, smooth out any air bubbles with fingers, a plastic card (like a credit card or supermarket card) or with a roller (brayer).

  For tissue paper and other lightweight papers, pour white glue in a clean dish and dilute it with about 20 percent water and mix with a brush. Then brush it on the section of the board you are covering and pat down the tissue paper on top. Roll out air bubbles starting from the center and rolling to each edge.

- **Permanent and Repositionable Glue Stick.** Rub the glue stick all over the back of the cut piece of paper, paying special attention to edges and corners. Set the glued object in place on the board and press out air bubbles and wrinkles as above. Permanent glue stick should stay in place. Repositionable glue stick allows you to paste up elements and then carefully remove

them if you decide to place them elsewhere.

- **Thick White Craft Glues.** I recommend Aleene's Tacky Glue or Sobo Craft & Fabric Glue. A few dots applied with a toothpick are enough for small items like dried flowers or single beads.

- **Spray Glue.** Try Tack2000 spray adhesive in a well-ventilated area, or outside on a day that's not windy. Spray on the section of the board you're using. Wait the recommended time, and then sprinkle small beads, sand, crystals, seeds, or other tiny elements and let them dry in place. Follow package directions.

- **Soft Gel Medium** (Matte). Golden is a good brand. Brush it on an area of your board that you want to cover with small items or brush on the back of larger elements you want to glue down. This is excellent for heavier or irregularly shaped elements, and it dries clear. It can be thinned with a little water if you've let the contents of the jar get dried out.

- **Polyurethane Glue.** Look for Gorilla Glue. Less is more with this strong adhesive. Apply it sparingly to an item, position the item on the board, and hold it in place for thirty seconds. Follow all package directions.

- **Glue Dots.** Zots Adhesive Dots come in various sizes on a roll and are used one or two at a time for small individual elements. Follow package directions.

- **Double-Sided Tape.** Use this for adhering mat board to a cardboard backing. You can use this generously.

- **Hot Glue Gun.** Use this for attaching pods and cones.

- **Other Ideas.** If glue fails and you're desperate to make something stick to your picture, try one of the following methods. It's not necessary to always hide these mechanics; in fact, they can often provide a decorative element to the picture. Try photo corners, stamp hinges, press-on Velcro, staples, tacks, nails, pushpins, needle and thread, wire, or cord.

Brushes

You'll need several sizes of brushes for both glue and paint. Get a $1^{1}/_{2}$-inch brush for spreading large sections of your board with glue and either a $^{1}/_{2}$-inch or $^{1}/_{4}$-inch brush for small sections or small papers. Wash brushes carefully after each art session, so that you'll be rewarded with a soft brush when you restart a project a day or a week later.

If you plan to paint papers, you can use these and others for finer work.

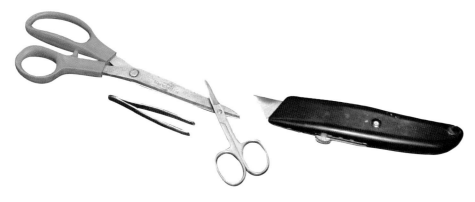

Cutting Tools

Use a craft knife, such as X-Acto, for cutting corrugated cardboard, mat board, and foam core to size. Use a cutting mat as a surface to cut against. You'll also use paper scissors, manicure scissors for small papers, all-purpose kitchen shears or garden shears for branches, wire cutters, fabric scissors, or pinking shears. When I first started doing collage, I found all of these around the house.

Board

The background of your collage, upon which all items are attached, is your board. In deciding which type to use, think of the strength and the color. Heavy elements need a strong background. You may plan to cover the board completely with your papers or incorporate its color into your design. On p. 117, I used a pale green mat board I found around the house, cut for some other use thirteen years

prior, because I liked the color for my spring tree.

Corrugated cardboard is ubiquitous and free. Cut the desired size and shape from a used carton. In your hunt for materials, you might find (or purchase) thin wood sheets, foam core in different colors, Masonite, mat board, or other strong cardboards. At art supply stores, you can get prepared canvas and clay board used for painting, but that is also good for collage. Ready-made frames sometimes come with precut cardboard and mats that you can use.

Also try heavy paper such as watercolor paper or Bristol Plate as your board. You'll need to lay the finished collage on heavier cardboard for support.

If your glue is quite wet and the cardboard thin, it might buckle as you work. When you've finished the project, turn it over, and with a big brush

and water, paint a large X from corner to corner and a fat line through the middle, and then weigh it down with heavy books until dry. The cardboard should flatten itself in the process.

Frames and Mats

For my very first collage, I cut a piece of corrugated cardboard as the teacher instructed, made something I liked, and wanted to frame and keep it. I was chagrined to learn that the size of my project couldn't fit in any ready-made frame, and I would have to pay a nice chunk of change to have it custom-framed. I learned my lesson quickly and now usually cut my board to standard sizes, such as 16 x 20 or 12 x 16, or select a frame in advance and incorporate the frame as part of the overall design.

Obviously your collage can be any shape you decide. *Building Bridges*

(page 48) is cut to emphasize the shape of the architecture, and the board is then floated on top of a rectangular mat, rather than have the mat cut out to match the collage. I can hang it this way or put it in a big rectangular frame.

Shadow boxes are fun and easy to use. They supply both the frame and the board simultaneously, and you know what you're working with from the start. See *Bird Box* on page 125 and *Grandma's Sewing Box* on page 28.

A Note about Acid

When original art is framed, professional framers recommend acid-free mat board, also called museum board or photo-safe material. Artist supplies are mostly acid-free, and you can find acid-free glues and construction paper as well. This helps to prevent fading and damage to the finished work. But in this book I'm using found materials—rusted bottle caps, newsprint, wire, foil, circuit boards, recycled papers, and small boxes. Who knows how they're made or what they contain.

I've decided to follow the advice of my esteemed teacher, Jerilyn Jurinek, and just relax and accept whatever process happens, as it's impossible to control. Newspaper and photos all fade over time. The newsprint that Pablo Picasso used in his collages one hundred years ago is now quite brown in tone, but looks amazing. Picasso knew that newspaper turns brown, but he used it anyway. Who am I to disagree?

Frames and mats are actually a part of the composition; any artwork is transformed by a frame and mat, so choose with an eye for what the overall piece should look like. In *The Garden in Winter* (page 115), I tried both a white mat, which enhances the icy feel, and a green mat, which encloses the scene and empowers the evergreens. Which would you choose?

Other Helpful Supplies

The following items can also be useful for enhancing a collage.

- Pencils and erasers
- Gold or silver pens
- Black Sharpie markers of different sizes
- Watercolor paint set
- Acrylic paints
- Pastels and chalk
- Ruler or T square

How to Do It

Artful collage is a six-step process: gathering, imagining, manipulating, designing, adhering, and displaying. The steps do not always follow in that exact order; for instance, sometimes imagining comes before gathering, or manipulating may come before imagining. The following sequence, however, will be helpful for getting started.

Gathering

While it's possible to buy interesting and beautiful papers and bags of craft supplies from the scrapbooking department of craft stores, I start from the premise that many of the artistic elements (as opposed to glues, boards, and tools) will come from stuff already at home using my 3R policy: Recycle, Repurpose and Reuse. Other materials will come from friends, family, and gracious people whom I ask to share or who offer supplies. Some people not only offer but beg you to take fabric remnants, ribbon, travel labels, and

such, because they want to be surprised by the artistic treatment of the mundane, offering a view that they never saw before, or because they want to clean out a drawer.

Don't discount stuff found at the curb on trash day on top of the cans or plastic bags, begging to be picked up and reused. If you're lucky, you have a town dump where there's a swap shed. Bring any useful item you don't want, take away any items free, no questions asked. Seek out yard sales for frames, boxes, and other treasures.

In addition to papers listed on p. 11, look among your sewing supplies, button boxes, and drawers of fabric, leather, yarn, ribbon, hardware nails and screws, twine, spices, costume jewelry, and beads. You can use sturdy foods like nuts, peppercorns, whole allspice, cloves, star anise, cinnamon sticks, whole nutmeg, barley, split peas, raw pumpkin and sunflower seeds, hard candies, colored sugars, and colored eggshells. Anything can work, such as broken pottery and dishes for mosaics; shoelaces, feathers, and men's ties for fabric; old computer cords and earbud connectors, candle stubs, thin and thick wire, bendable copper tubing, old and new sandpaper, shells, dried seaweed, or driftwood. The list is endless and part of the fun is in the hunt.

Stockpile more than you need to allow creative choices as you work. Start saving tissue paper from gift boxes, as well as the small boxes themselves. While you watch a favorite program, gather the day's junk mail, catalogs, newspaper, and magazines and cut out any pages with great color, texture, or fonts. I rip out and save a lot of sky images because I like to create collages of cityscapes.

You will see your trash in a whole new light. Inevitably, you will see your surroundings as a potential treasure trove as you gather ordinary material for reuse in an entirely different context.

Imagining

Imagine what you could create, what you'd like to express. Sometimes imagining comes before gathering, sometimes after. I visualize the art I want to make, daydream over the possibilities, think about it while showering, and then deliberately go out and seek the materials I need. Sometimes there's a full-blown theme, but sometimes a type of material comes your way and you have to build an idea around that. That's called the "demand quality" of objects. Something will grab you and make you use it in a certain way, as the honeycomb packing paper did for me in *Under Water* (see page 72).

I have a friend who wants to make a birthday collage for the adult daughter who has everything. I suggested gathering old snapshots, pieces of artwork from when the daughter was young, her initials cut or torn from discarded printed matter, images depicting her interest in dancing, letters spelling out her various schools—again an endless list of possibilities. The birthday girl's sisters can help with the hunt; they have their own items that could be part of a great collage.

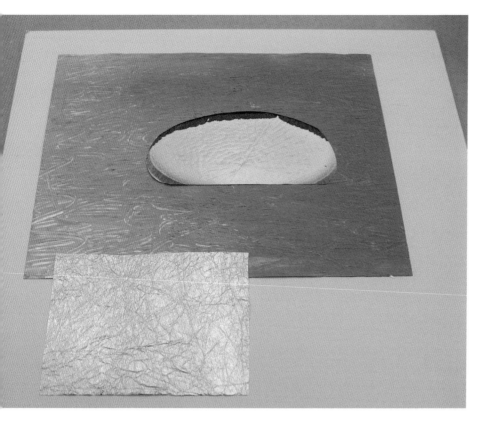

sacrifice! But I don't find the triangular boxes until months later when I wait for a train in Boston's South Station. There they are at Regina Pizzeria, in business since 1926. But by the time I find them, I've already switched my allegiance to the round wood boxes containing Camembert cheese. I have plenty of these.

Still, though I no longer need them, I revert back to the gathering stage and start collecting discarded triangular pizza boxes from tables in South Station. I look for those without a lot of cheese and tomato paste stuck to them. I have no shame. I politely ask people who have finished their slice if I could collect the box for an art project. They smile and think I'm a little strange, but I'm nicely dressed, so maybe I'm telling the truth. No one refuses. Someday I'll really need those boxes.

One of the papers that my granddaughter Annabelle hand-painted reminded me so much of Monet's water lily paintings (which she has never seen) that I needed to make a collage based on that thought. In this case, the material came first, and then I imagined the rest.

Here's another example of imagining. I plan to make a collage color wheel for this book, with eight pie-shaped segments. I start to gather colored papers cut from newsprint, magazines, and flyers for this color wheel. I'm dreaming about using triangular boxes that individual pizza slices sometimes come in; they'll be perfect to contain each color. I live within walking distance of about forty pizza shops in Manhattan. Which one uses the boxes I envision? The hunt is on. I can hardly wait to find the right shop. I've already decided to order a cheese and mushroom slice with extra peppers so I can start with my collage plan. My husband and three friends are joining in the search. What

Manipulating

You can use materials exactly as they have been gathered, only cutting off the proper size for your purpose, or you can transform them to tell another story. Some of my favorite manipulations involve antiquing an element in the design. You probably have supplies for dying with tea bags or instant coffee. Make a cup of super strong beverage, paint or dab on the surface of your collage element with a brush, and let it dry. Or smear a damp tea bag or coffee grounds directly on your picture to achieve the desired look.

To antique metal, soak a piece of steel wool (the kind without soap) in a dish with an inch of water for a few days. Turn it daily until both the steel wool and the water turn rusty. Paint the rusty water on your collage element and let it dry.

Scorch paper or fabric with a hot iron, or singe edges with a candle, being careful not to set things aflame. Practice on a scrap piece before you do this to your good material. You may have done this in grade school when you wanted to make a treasure map appear ancient.

With some elements, you can bend, cut, tear, fringe, cut off pieces, roll, stretch, crumple, crease, flatten, iron smooth, pleat, coil, spiral, hammer, or stretch. You can add paint, crayon, pastel, chalk, pencil, ink, or dye.

Paint and stamp your own papers to use in other collages. Use vegetables and fruits for stamping, or use manufactured stamps that you buy. Onions cut in half make beautiful stamps when you brush the cut half with some acrylic paint.

Designing

After imagining how your collage will look, gathering the materials, and manipulating them, you must design your project by actually laying it out on your board. Once it is pasted down, you have very little wiggle room for correction, so this is an important step.

When you have the piece designed to your satisfaction, but not yet glued in place, slide all of your elements onto another board or tray. That way you'll remember how you wanted to place things as you glue the elements in layers.

Famous collage artist Esteban Vincente worked with his board propped upright on an easel and pinned his elements (mostly paper) to his board. He could then change positions of elements as he walked by the collage in his studio over a period of many weeks.

Working vertically allows you to see your piece from the vantage point of its final placement, usually upright on a wall, mantel, or shelf. It looks very different when you're looking down on it. I work flat on a table, but as soon as I can, I prop up my piece to see what needs doing next, and I always look at it that way before I declare it finished.

Sometimes when designing, you realize you need more stuff, or something different, and must go back to gathering. American artist Jasper Johns said about art, "Take an object. Do something to it. Do something else to it." I often think of this as I'm working; knowing when to stop "doing something else" is an art in itself.

For each project in this book, I describe the design tips and techniques for that project. So flip through those sections for ideas you can incorporate into your own work. Here are some examples:

- Glue elements on top of each other, layering them either partially, or fully obscuring materials below, and create a third dimension.

- Vary smooth, rough, shiny, dull, and marbleized textures.

- Arrange pieces by color, size, and dark to light to see how they feel.

- Repeat color, shape, pattern, and texture for a more unified feel.

- Decide whether to cover the whole background or incorporate some of the background into your design.

- Incorporate parts of other art and craft work that you've done: bits of knitting, crochet, weaving, felted wool, pressed flowers, watercolor or oil sketches, or photographs (see *Grandma Roses* on page 88).

- Start gluing the biggest elements first, then medium elements, then smallest, or plan out everything at once and glue down the first layer, starting from the top of the page or the bottom, making things smaller for distance.

- Edit your work as you design. Sometimes adding more is just too much.

- Think about whether you want a 3-D effect, almost like relief or sculpture, or whether you want a flat effect (see *The Mask* on page 94).

- Cutting vs. tearing paper gives two different looks. Tearing printed papers, like magazine images, produces a different amount of white edge depending on whether you tear top-down or bottom-up. Experiment on a practice piece of the same paper and decide what you want.

- Your work can be tidy or rough.

- Extend work over the edge of the frame, mat, or board. You can make your image escape from the confines of the edges (see *Bird Box* on page 125).

- Begin with way more stuff than you need for finished work. Select as you go. Make full use of your copier or printer to supply images and fonts.

- Cut board the right size for a ready-made frame or a frame you already have. Be aware that odd-size boards lead to the extra expense of custom matting and framing.

- Do a series. Explore a favorite theme in several pictures. You'll develop your technique as you proceed. I did four cityscapes in different light and seasons for this book and figured out how I liked the sky as I went along. Some will be more successful than others. Remember that Monet painted the same water lily pond and the same cathedral numerous times to explore the scene and the changing light.

- Look for inspiration in museums, galleries, books, and online. Explore the work of other artists, such as Pablo Picasso's guitars, the collage and mixed media of Romare Bearden and Robert Rauschenberg, and the boxes of Joseph Cornell.

Adhering

I already discussed tools, materials, and methods for adhering the objects to the board in the previous chapter. After all the items are glued, pasted, wired, or in some other way secured to the piece, the next step is to decide how to display it.

Displaying

Before you do anything else, sign your work. You're the artist. Own up to it. Especially if you are giving the collage as a gift, your name should be a permanent part of the presentation.

Decide whether you want to frame your piece. Even if you frame it, however, you have many options for display other than mounting it on a wall. You can stand it on a mantelpiece, shelf, or desk, or lean it against a plate stand, music stand, or book stand.

Place your work out of direct sunlight to minimize fading. Keep it away from windows. An interior wall, shelf, or desk is best. If you're framing under glass, consider nonglare glass that has UV protection. As you're working, either balance the physical weight of elements in your picture to allow finished work to hang straight, or adjust for imbalance in the piece when adding the hanging hardware.

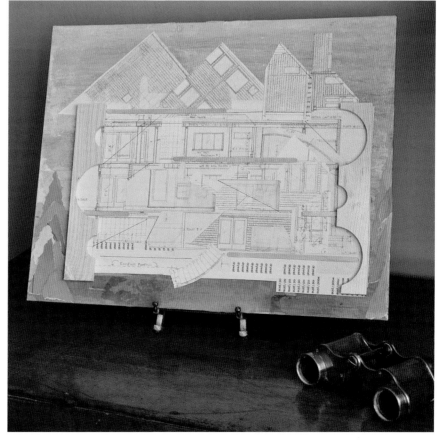

Projects

Many artists start with a limiting theme. It's rumored that famed New York City collagist Robert Rauschenberg sometimes chose the theme "what I find on the streets circumnavigating my block today."

In the following pages, ten themed sections are presented in no particular order. You can make similar collages for practice, or develop you own ideas based on the inspirations.

THEMED SECTIONS

Remembrance of Things Past

Design a collage with a specific person in mind. Make it a tribute, with ideas that refer to things he or she has done or things he or she likes. Present it as a gift for a birthday, Mother's Day, Father's Day, a graduation, a retirement, or other special occasion. Or create a collage for yourself as a memento of a special place, a time in your life, or of a historical era of particular interest to you.

PROJECT 1. Grandma's Sewing Box

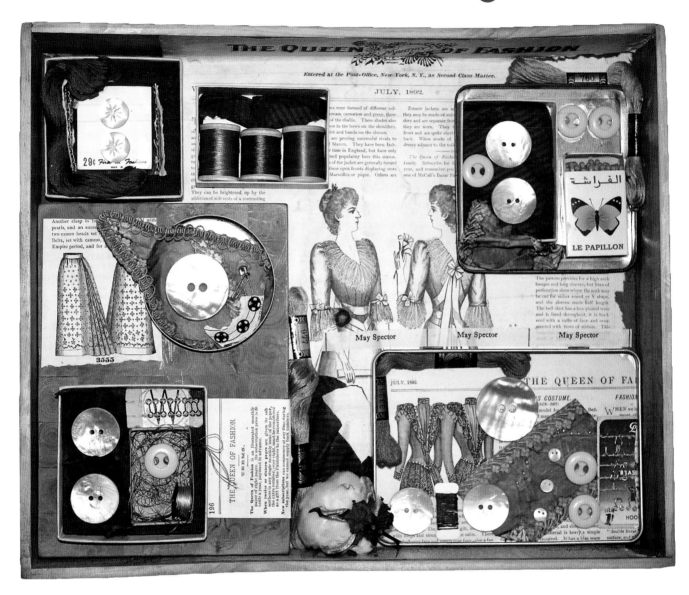

Materials: Assortment of small boxes and lids, pages from an 1892 fashion magazine, fabric scraps, spools of thread, bobbin, embroidery thread, buttons, name tags, cotton boll, and small empty boxes and lids. All items were found at home or donated by my son-in-law, an inveterate collector.

Background: Old wood box, 11½ x 14½ x 2 inches, found at the swap shed of a small-town dump.

Adhesives: White glue for paper, small boxes, and small elements. Gorilla Glue for metal boxes and the bigger wooden box.

Every female family member who sees this piece covets it. It's a combination, all-in-one scrapbook page and memory box honoring my mother, May Spector, with most of the elements coming from her old sewing box, which I inherited. My eight-year-old granddaughter offers the highest compliment: "Grammy, don't sell this one, because I want it."

I first gathered an assortment of small boxes. Wooden matchboxes are handy. You can use lids if the boxes themselves are too deep, or use the bottom and lid separately. Try out placement within the big box. I inverted the wooden box lid on the left to make a platform for other, smaller boxes.

I used a large page from a magazine or newspaper as part of the background, making sure important images will show. Some paper runs up the top and bottom sides of the big box.

I repositioned the small boxes as needed. After gluing on the newspaper background first, I then glued down the boxes, followed by the smaller elements.

PROJECT 2. My Field of Dreams

Materials: Cut and torn tissue paper, construction paper, newsprint images, painted paper, colored pencil.

Background: Acid free mat board, 17 x 20 inches.

Adhesives: Diluted white glue for the tissue paper; brush directly on the board, and then smooth out air bubbles, pressing gently with your hand so the paper won't tear. Soft gel medium (matte) for most other papers. For the large piece of green, because it's a heavy paper, brush on reverse side of paper and also on the board; position the paper and then smooth out air bubbles starting in the center. Use your hand or a brayer and continue to press from the center of the green to each edge, as you would roll out pie dough with a rolling pin. Glue stick for small pieces like the bases and scoreboard. Double-sided tape to float collage on a larger board for framing.

Fathers are known to introduce their sons to baseball. My father, a huge baseball fan, had only daughters. We'd listen to the Phillies and A's games on the radio, learn lineups and batting averages, and form images in our minds of how the game was played. One memorable hot summer evening, our dad took us to Shibe Park, then home to the Philadelphia Athletics. Decades later, the stunning image remains: darkening sky with setting sun, banks of lights bathing a field of unimaginable green, players

throwing balls for miles, billboards advertising Ballantine beer, Cracker Jack prizes, learning to keep score, and falling asleep in the car on the way home. What a night!

This collage leaps from a childhood memory. Much of it is surreal; accuracy is secondary. Proportions and distances are flexible. I did Google the team and stadium, however, to check on what they looked like the year I was there. The billboards feature three red balls, suggesting the Ballantine logo. Orange tissue cut in long streams represents the light streaming from the huge poles to bathe the field. Three players cut from newspapers represent the team.

I cut the sports fans in the stands from several newspapers and magazines, and then I gently added color with pencils to the group at bottom right.

The scoreboard I remembered was not a flashy electronic thing; the scores were posted by a man behind the board, reaching out and actually posting the numbers by hand. The collage is made of many layers, and it is important to glue down papers in a particular order so they will be visible at the end. I will describe the papers in the order I glued them down.

- Tissue paper of dark blue and lavender for the sky.

- Large green square for the infield and outfield grass.

- Torn strips of paper I painted for streaks of sunset.

- Brown papers purchased for dirt beyond the field; I tore a rough edge on the paper to represent the unevenness of the dirt.

- Green papers purchased for grass outside the third-base line.

- Diminishing sizes of paper rectangles for the billboards; the tops are cut in a slant to create the illusion of distance.

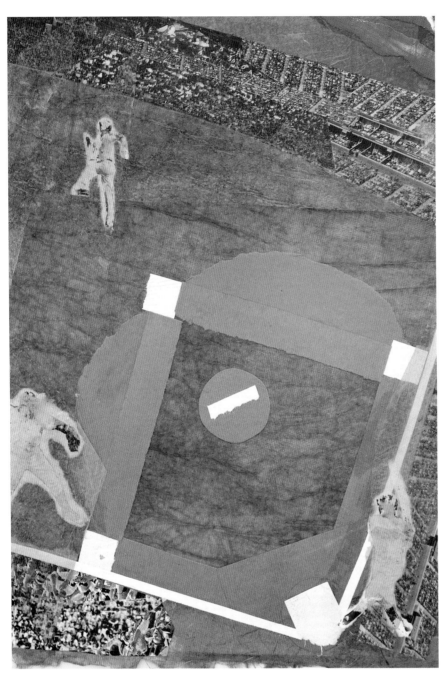

- Red paper circles on the billboards for the beer logo, also in diminishing sizes.

- Brown construction paper for the batter's box, infield dirt, and pitcher's mound.

- Textured paper purchased for bases, home plate, and pitcher's rubber.

- Two thin strips of white construction paper for the foul lines.

- Black construction paper for light standards above billboards.

- Green paper rectangle for the scoreboard; then on top, a rectangle of paper with small squares, and then the word "scoreboard" cut from the sports page of a newspaper.

- Cut pieces of fans in the stands along first and third base and left field.

- Cut and torn pictures from newspapers of three players at home, first base, and outfield.

- Flag in leftfield.

- Streaming from the light poles and the stands

- Triangles of golden and orange tissue paper bathing the men and some of the field in light.

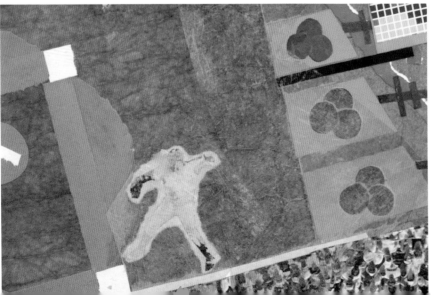

PROJECT 3. A Room with a View

Materials: Construction paper, colored paper from magazines, and buttons—all found at home; recycled coffee stirring sticks and acrylic paint. The construction paper is from a packet my grandchildren have used for years; dull colors like gray, brown, and black are always the last to be selected, languishing in my closet until rescued here.

Background: Acid-free mat board, 11 1/2 x 14.

Adhesives: Glue stick for papers and thick white craft glue for the buttons and sticks.

This collage is a tribute to Simba the cat. It's been twenty years since my son adopted her off the streets of Woburn, Massachusetts, and gave her a loving home. Now she needs help to climb on a high stool or bed, but she still loves to peer out the window and sun herself in the warmth. She's quick to turn herself away from the family to view more enticing scenes outdoors.

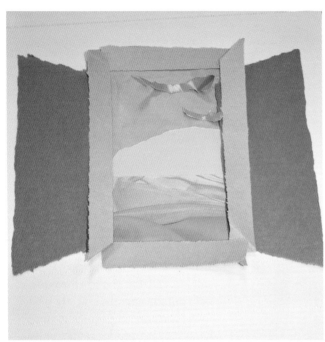

All of the paper is torn, not cut, lending a rough appeal, and in the case of Simba, a furry look to her coat. First I tore four pieces of magazine paper for the view out the window.

Then I measured and creased gray paper for a window frame and tore on the folded lines. I measured and creased the light blue construction paper for the shutters, tearing the top and bottom edges on slants to give the window the illusion of depth. This perspective applies only to the shutters, yet dominates the whole scene.

After tearing the rest of the pieces of paper, gathering the other materials, and trying them, I glued them down in this order: outside scene, window frame, shutters, detail on shutters (stir sticks), stool, tail and legs, cat body, and shutter knobs (buttons). For the window frame, I glued down the top and bottom and then bent the corners of the two side pieces to make them look like a carpenter's miter joint.

The cat is huge in comparison to the window, but all cats think they are super-important, and she is, after all, the inspiration. This collage hung in my office for three months while I was working on my book. The white background, which I had liked at first, began to bother me. Options for wallpaper are restricted after the fact, but I thought sponge painting might work.

My sponge is not the traditional natural one, but a small rectangle of clean Scotch-Brite scour pad.

I mixed a gray color, dipped the pad in the paint, and then stamped it on the background. The texture is just what I wanted. For tight spaces use an edge of the pad. After the gray fully dried I added another color on top.

PROJECT 4. Write Me

Materials: Cover and pages from out-of-date passport, letters, new and canceled postage stamps, autograph from horticulturist J. C. Raulston, stamps from Everglades National Park, torn and cut papers with various calligraphy, old Esterbrook fountain pen—all found at home.

Background: Reused mat and 20 x 16-inch frame, found at home. Note that the mat shows remnants of old glue. These are covered in the new collage.

Adhesives: White glue for heavier papers; apply glue to both the object and the section of the mat where the paper will lay. Glue stick for light papers. Gorilla Glue for the pen. If mat buckles from moisture in the glue, weigh down completed sections with a small stack of books until the board dries.

Although I mean to keep a very uncluttered home, how can I resist hiding away my long out-of-date passport, an envelope from a granddaughter addressed merely to Grammy and Bum, a fan letter from a reader in Brazil, and some proof stamps from my recent trip to Everglades National Park? Why do I still have a six-cent first class envelope when I'm not really a stamp collector? That ink pen that I once used to write with in college, did it really have to follow me through eight moves? Here's a collage that is truly a one-page scrapbook, taking me through a long series of wonderful memories.

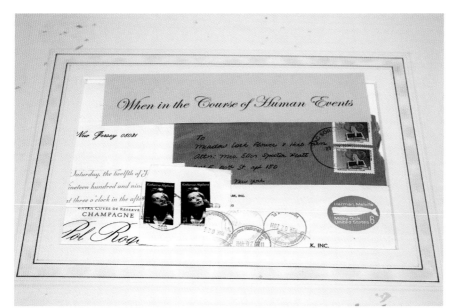

The mat had been beautifully cut and lined in the past, but had residual spots of glue from previous use. In the current design, I used both the interior rectangle and the entire top surface of the mat as background.

All of the calligraphy was cut or torn from items I received in the mail or from newspapers, but I printed "When in the Course of Human Events" from my home computer, feeding old paper into my printer. My iMac comes with a selection of hundreds of fonts and a range of sizes; here I used 48-point Edwardian Script. Using this beautiful frame that was already in my possession, there was not enough depth for both the pen and covering glass. I chose to add the pen and discard the glass. An alternative would be to buy a shadow box frame.

PROJECT 5. Rusty Memories

Materials: Old license plate, rusty nails, bottle caps, copper plant-row markers, pennies, buttons, brass star ornaments, museum admission buttons, metal picture frame, recycled red paper bag—all found at home; and chicken wire.

Background: Shadow box frame, 9 x 20 inches, with its own Masonite board.

Adhesives: Gorilla Glue for chicken wire. Wrapped wire for license plate. Glue dots for museum buttons and small items. White glue for red paper.

The central element in this piece is the truck license plate from my flower and herb farm, The Meadow Lark. Not every collage must be pretty. Here I'm going for the rusty farm look, including chicken wire.

I cut chicken wire to size. It was newly purchased, so to make it look old, I painted the wire with very strong rust solution. I did the same with the museum buttons, and then let them dry. I glued a piece of cut red paper bag to almost cover the Masonite and then attached the chicken wire.

Even though the license plate with its road dirt was the central element, it seemed too dominant; so with a tin snips, I made two cuts to each side and bent the cuts upward.

I then attached license plate to the chicken wire with small pieces of wire poked through the screw holes. Next, I attached pieces of metal picture frame and then smaller items to the background, trying for a 3-D effect where possible. I pleated a piece of red paper bag to give even more depth.

PROJECT 6. Temple of the Gods

Materials: Advertising yardstick, birch bark, birch twigs, tan packing paper, two golden epaulettes, chopsticks, cut papers, sun ornament, gold thread—all found at home; and photograph of carving on furniture, brown textured paper, gold spray paint.

Background: Shallow wooden box/frame, 13½ x 13½ inches.

Adhesives: Soft gel matte medium for yardstick, chopsticks, and papers. Smooth out large papers with a brayer or plastic card as you go. Hot glue gun for twigs and bark.

The idea for this project came from the intricate carving on a sideboard I own and then finding a box/frame curbside on trash day and coincidentally noticing the folding yardstick among my stuff. With the advertising side of the yardstick face down, it just fit inside the box—

maybe a sign from the collage gods. The tan packing paper at the top of the frame is courtesy of my supermarket, which wraps such paper around egg cartons for home delivery. After you've done a few collage pieces, the whole world seems to supply you with treasures.

I photographed some intricate carving on my sideboard, printed it out on plain paper, and then cut it to size.

I glued the brown textured paper first and then cut the photo for the background. Then I positioned the yardstick and glued it down.

I added the sun ornament next, because it helped direct me in the design. Two pairs of chopsticks form the door to the inner sanctum and all the rest follows in a balanced way, though the two sides aren't identical. It was only after finishing the project that I wanted gold on the yardstick, chopsticks, and woven paper. Since I had only spray paint on hand, I went outside with the whole project, sprayed a small pool of paint into an old jar lid, and brushed the paint wherever I wanted it.

My Landscape, My World

My city, New York, holds endless fascination with its ever-changing vistas. But my world also encompasses my state, country, backyard, rooftop, office, favorite reading chair, and so. Start with a theme in your world and the ideas will come pouring in.

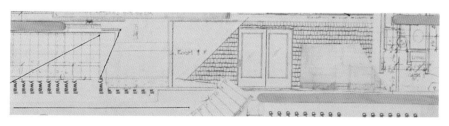

PROJECT 7. Water Towers, New York City

Materials: Cut images from magazines and newspapers, sheet music, two photographs printed on plain paper, pressed leaves, painted papers—all found at home; and oil pastels.

Background: Corrugated cardboard, 16 x 20 inches.

Adhesives: Diluted white glue for all the papers. Dabs of Aleene's Tacky Glue for the pressed leaves.

I used to live in the country, with a view of the rolling hills of north-eastern Pennsylvania. Now I live in New York City with a view from my living room window of water towers, air-conditioning units, and a few green rooftops. I've come to love this industrial scene as it represents the city, my home.

The light changes with the weather and the time of day. I watch how the setting sun bounces off the water towers toward evening. I hung out of my fifteenth-story window to take photographs in the early morning and early evening. I printed out two images on plain paper and used other cut papers to form my own city landscape.

I measured the size of the mat and frame and marked the board in pencil, so that I'll know the confines of this picture. I then placed the two large photos first, slightly overlapping, and checked to see that they lined up in some meaningful way before I glued them down. The buildings are easier to place, as they all are glued on in layers.

I cut pieces of sheet music, painted papers, and magazine photos of brick and stone into fanciful building shapes and placed them on the surface of the photos; several cover the seam where the two photos meet. I tore blue newsprint to form clouds. I wanted to landscape some city rooftops so I colored some with two shades of green oil pastels before I started gluing small bits of shrubs and trees. My last task was to "plant" a few trees at street level, which I formed from pressed Japanese maple leaves.

PROJECT 8. Night on the Town, New York City

Materials: Five digital images printed on plain paper, gold fabric, gold paper from a chocolate bar, gold metal band, cut paper—all found at home; and gold ink.

Background: Corrugated cardboard and precut mat, 20 x 16 inches.

Adhesives: Diluted white glue for all the papers and fabric; smooth out air bubbles from each piece before adding the next. Gorilla Glue for the metal strip.

In my friend Fran's building in New York there is a sky lounge on the thirty-first floor with a balcony, and we often gather to play a competitive game of bridge as the light streams in and the whole West Side is laid out before us. I can't resist bringing my camera and shooting 180 degrees of architecture as the sun is setting and the building lights are coming on. This collage is more about feeling than accuracy. New Yorkers who know the West Side are disoriented when they recognize individual buildings, but notice that something is "wrong" about the placement.

I cut all of the sky away from the photos, silhouetting the buildings. I cut out my favorite buildings and placed the largest in position, then the smaller ones in layers, trying lots of arrangements before I was satisfied. Before gluing the buildings, I formed the sky from several different torn pieces of dark blue newsprint (from various ads). The sky must be glued down first, then the tallest buildings, and then shorter ones toward the bottom of the page. I cut and added fabric for the peaked roofs and gold foil and metal strip to represent car lights on the streets. Near the bottom right, I formed dots with the gold ink pen to mimic window lights.

PROJECT 9. Up at the Met

Materials: Two photographs printed on plain paper, birds and butterflies scanned from books, pressed leaves and flowers, colored pencils.

Background: Corrugated cardboard, 10½ x 24 inches, floated on mat board and framed.

Adhesives: Diluted white glue for the big images, glue stick for the small bits, and dabs of Aleene's Tacky Glue for the flower and leaves. Use a toothpick to handle the Tacky Glue.

It's Members' Day at the Metropolitan Museum of Art, walking distance from my home. I want to take advantage of the big shop discount and the free tea and cookies they have laid out on this normally closed Monday. I sit in the Great Hall sipping my tea and nibbling on a huge oatmeal cookie in the quiet. My eyes scan the ceiling and I'm treated to a view I normally rush past in the crowds: the huge domes and arches of this grand space. I had no intention of taking photos, but of course my camera was over my shoulder, so

I took shots of these grand architectural elements. I fantasized about birds nesting beneath the dome and butterflies flitting by.

There are two images here, one in the center. The second I printed twice and inverted for the two side panels, creating a new Great Hall. I scanned images of birds and butterflies, cut them out, and used colored pencils ad lib. I glued down the three big photographs first and then the birds and butterflies. A few pressed flowers and leaves complete the scene.

PROJECT 10. Building Bridges

Materials: Cut digital images, torn and painted construction paper, watercolor paint, and gold pen.
Background: Foam core, 12 x 22 inches.
Adhesives: Permanent glue stick. Leave extra paper to wrap around the sides of foam if the cut edges are rough.

Like Robert Moses and other ambitious city designers, I can build my own bridges and cityscapes, restructuring the skyline using only a few digital images, watercolors, and pens. Here, the iconic Brooklyn Bridge is presented in three main images taken from three different vantage points, including one from a boat in the middle of the East River.

First I measured and marked the foam core to the desired shape and size with a light pencil and cut it with a sharp craft knife against a ruler. Then I painted the river in each image a more vivid shade of blue than ever seen in New York. Because the photos were taken in different lights, the paint helped unify the final image. Next I laid out the design of the major images and cut where I felt necessary. Sometimes I cut out the sky from the image and pasted the remaining bridge structure on a newly constructed sky. I printed out extra water or sky as necessary to fill in. With a gold pen I connected bridge cables from image to image. I found extra pieces of water not only added horizontal and vertical shapes, they covered a water taxi, traffic lights, and cars that I wanted to edit out.

PROJECT 11. Design/Build

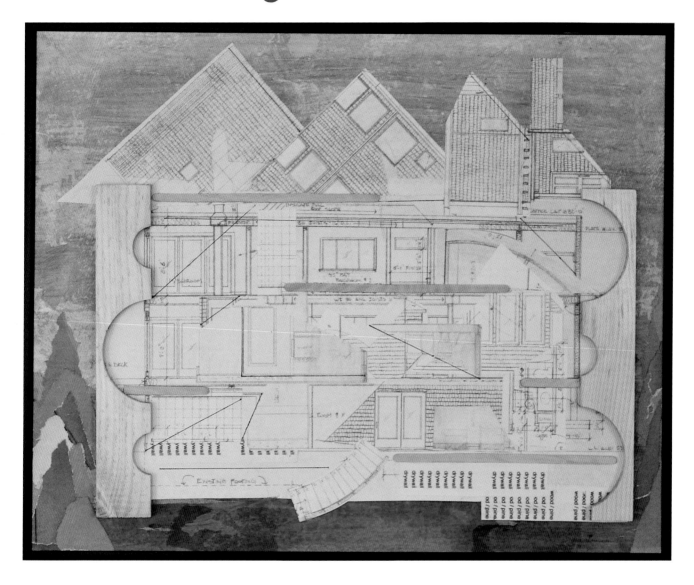

Materials: Torn green newsprint, white tissue paper, stir sticks, inserts from a wooden wine crate—all found at home; blueprints from an architect friend; and ink, acrylic paint, sidewalk chalk.

Background: Canvas board, 16 x 20 inches.

Adhesives: Thinned white glue or glue stick for cut pieces of blueprint and green newsprint, torn to represent trees. For heavier wooden elements, brush on a coat of soft matte gel medium on the underside, press down on top of the papers, and weigh down until glue dries.

What I imagined would be a study in constructing a house evolved into a self-contained miniature dollhouse. Would you add a dog by the front door? Some children? Furniture? It's all up to the artist. For now, I'll leave it for the viewer's imagination to fill in, though I certainly might make additions a month or year from now.

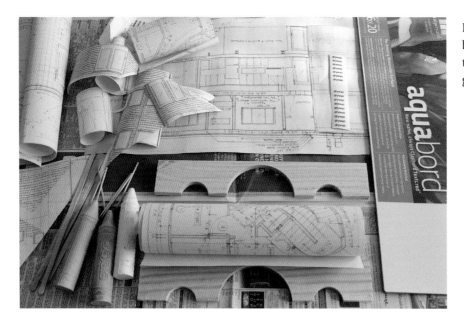

From two large pages of discarded blueprints, I cut the pieces that had the most interesting lines and reorganized them into a fanciful building.

The roof is composed of four triangles of different sizes and angles and one rectangle for the chimney. The wooden wine crate inserts form the outside walls of the house and add the arches. Stir sticks roughly separate the floors.

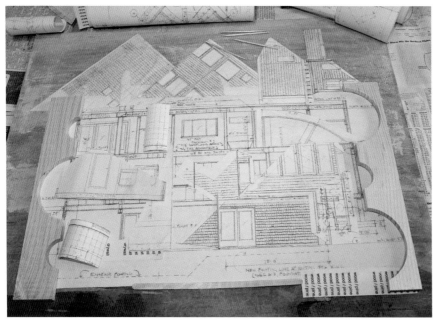

I painted blue sky and let it dry. Then I rubbed on paler blue chalk to give texture and tone down the color. It was still too bright, so I brushed diluted white glue directly on the painted canvas and added white tissue on top. With a roller and then my fingers, I smoothed it out. The tissue was fragile so I used a light touch.

Even though I've designed gardens professionally, I've chosen not to landscape the front of the house, leaving the wild evergreens to stand on their own. I rubbed light blue chalk to cover some of the cut pieces of blueprint, and wiped off the excess with a clean paper towel.

PROJECT 12. A Child's Skyline

Materials: Cut paper all found at home; and watercolor paints.
Background: White Bristol Board, 11 x 14 inches.
Adhesives: Diluted white glue.

I had no intention of making this skyline so childlike, but the colors I chose made it happen.

I painted the top of the paper a vivid blue and painted some other pieces of white paper and sheet music to use for buildings. Then I cut skyscrapers with peaked, slanted, and flat roofs, even a water tower, and then layered them on. The farthest buildings I glued down first, near the top of the page; the closer ones I glued on later. Pressed leaves represent street trees and a roof garden. Torn pieces of foil and dark blue paper are positioned last.

Color Coded

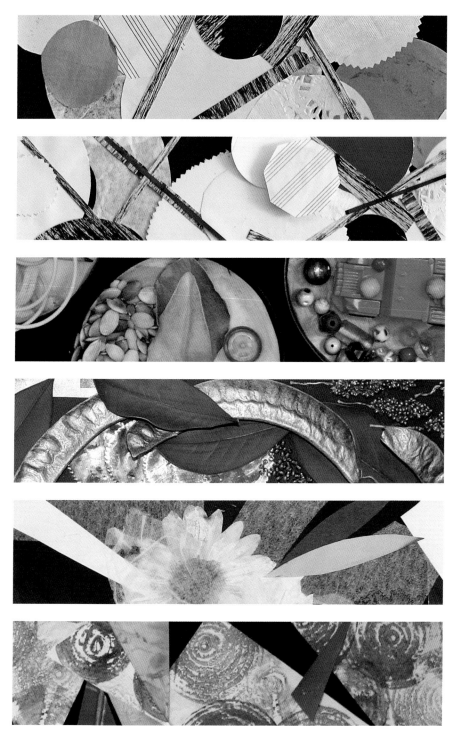

Color can be a major theme. Limit your palette to a select group of colors. See how it unifies your collage. Try black and white, all pastels, all primary colors, jewel tones, or whatever color combinations come to mind.

PROJECT 13. Black and White

Materials: Cut paper, coffee filter, paper doily, used sanding disc—all found at home; and black gesso, watercolor paper. For *Black and White and Red All Over*, three red paper circles of different sizes and five red paper strips—all found at home.

Background: Corrugated cardboard, 17 x 23 inches.

Adhesives: Diluted white glue. For the red variation, repositionable glue stick for the red elements, giving me the option of removing them easily if I liked the first version better.

PROJECT 14. Black and White and Red All Over

The New York City Ballet Company dancing *La Source*, choreographed by the late great George Balanchine, inspired the lines and circles here. Upon seeing the first steps, I felt a sharp, involuntary intake of my breath; the ballet was quite literally breathtaking to view. Although the ballerinas' tutus were in shades of shell pink, I wanted the clarity of only black and white.

After finishing *Black and White*, I viewed it for a month and then decided to add some bold color. A friend who viewed this work in progress said it looked like "an aerial view of a jazz scene—lots of movement and gaiety." Red will do that to you every time.

First, I painted a sheet of watercolor paper with gesso using a dry brush and let it dry. Then I cut out some circles with a big scissors and narrow strips with a paper cutter.

I drew circles of different sizes by tracing round objects like glasses and bowls; the kitchen is a great place to find lots of circles. Then I cut the circles with scissors, or used pinking shears for diverse edges. Or you can fold a circle in half, then in half again, and then once more, leaving you with a piece the shape of a pie wedge. Cut off the rounded bottom of the wedge, leaving a straight edge, and unfold. Here there are 23 circles and 8 strips. I glued the largest elements first, interspersing the strips and circles, so that the strips are not all on the top layer. I overlapped elements as I placed them.

For *Black and White and Red All Over*, I was able to slip a red circle under a white one where the glue hadn't held. The red strips all follow near or on top of one of the black and white strips to prevent too much chaos. The red has great power to transform the collage so only a few pieces are needed.

Since this is an abstract, try looking at the finished work both vertically and horizontally (the way I made it). Either way can work. See which way you like best.

PROJECT 15. Wheelie

Materials: Small boxes from Camembert cheese, a variety of objects found at home (see below), cut papers in various colors, black gesso.

Background: Wooden cheese box from whole brie, begged from a cheese shop, painted with black gesso, 14½ inch diameter.

Adhesives: Papers attached with white glue or glue stick and heavier elements, like shells and blue car, with drops of Gorilla Glue, pressing in place for a minute until the bond forms. For intermediate weight items, such as the bottoms of the round boxes, Tacky Glue was brushed on for adhering to the big round box.

The color wheel displays a series of mini collages made of small items found in the back of a junk drawer, tool bench, button tin, toy box, and other nooks and crannies around the house. I started each one with cut colored paper from newspapers or magazines and then tried to have different materials represent each color.

I nested the top and bottom of the large circular box to make it sturdier and painted it and the smaller box tops and bottoms with black gesso and let them all dry.

Then I gathered the materials and placed them in the boxes. It took some time to amass everything for each color.

I strived for a three-dimensional effect, with some items coming up to the rim or even slightly over.

Red: Pushpins, rubber bands, red wire.

Orange: Buttons, strips of dried orange rind.

Yellow: Pencils, pipe cleaners, wire.

Blue: Beads, car from cereal box.

Green: Lids from floral water tubes, raw pumpkin seeds, salal leaf.

Purple: Felt, rubber bands, shoelace, dried delphinium flowers, M&Ms.

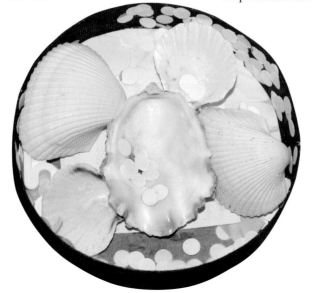

White: Shells, plastic wall mounts, punch paper dots.

PROJECT 16. The Crown Jewels

Materials: Locust pods, acorns, small cones, magnolia leaves, newsprint, heads of paper fasteners, tiny beads, legal seals, copper ring—all found at or near home; and copper and gold spray paint, sorghum stems.

Background: Shadow box frame with its own black board, 17 x 20 inches.

Adhesives: Diluted white glue for the paper mosaic tiles and seals. White glue full strength for the paper fasteners and beads. Hot glue gun and glue sticks for pods, cones, and leaves. Gorilla Glue for the copper ring.

In fall, when big locust pods dropped down to decorate city sidewalks near my home, I gathered some to form a collage necklace. I hunted for other "jewels" in the park and in my craft closet. Anything sprayed gold, silver, or copper assumes the luster of precious metal, even the newspaper I used to protect my work surface during paint spraying.

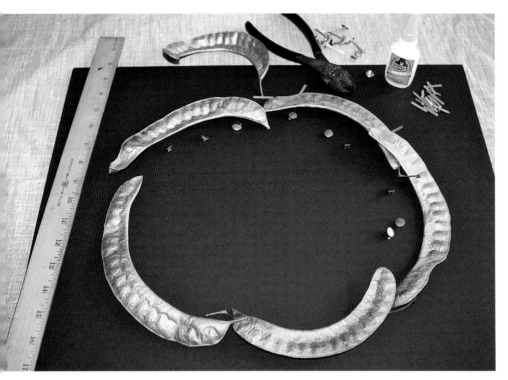

After gathering the simple elements I spray painted them copper or gold, but left the acorns and the magnolia leaves their natural colors. With a wire cutter, I removed the prongs of the paper fasteners. After spraying the gold and copper items, I cut up newspaper used as paint protection into small mosaic tiles and used the tiles as part of the dcsign.

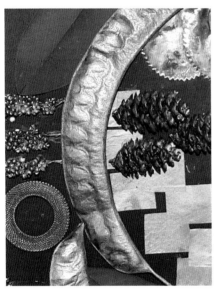

PROJECT 17. Still Life with Black and White

Sun streamed in the window, bathing an empty vase on a table. A few other objects were scattered around. My assignment was to create a collage from this scene, emphasizing black and white.

Here I glued the vase down first and then the table on top and overlapping. The table was cut from mottled black paper, and I glued white tissue paper on top. By not smoothing out the tissue, I made the table look marbleized. I added three pressed flowers, three pressed leaves, leaves in gray tones cut from paper, and some falling petals. Though the collage is not strictly black and white, the heart-shaped leaves of the elephant ear come pretty close. The centers of the daisies had faded quite a bit from their natural yellow, so I painted them with yellow watercolors. When painting flowers, I add a tiny drop of liquid detergent to the paint to make it stick. Bright white triangles represent the sunlight. Other pieces of white and black paper were added where needed. Postage stamps decorate the vase, because this issue of Katharine Hepburn is all black and white.

Materials: Torn and cut papers, music composition paper, pressed Montauk daisies, elephant ear leaves, canceled postage stamps, lens cleaning tissue, tissue paper—all found at home; and yellow watercolor paint.
Background: Black cardboard, 11 x 14 inches.
Adhesives: Diluted white glue for the papers and dabs of Aleene's Tacky Glue for the leaves and flowers.

PROJECT 18. What's Your Angle?

Materials: Black gesso, painted papers.
Background: Cardboard painted with a coat of black gesso. The frame, one that I reused from another project, is 7 x 28 inches.
Adhesives: All of the pieces are glued onto the painted cardboard backing with permanent glue stick.

My angle was helping my two granddaughters, ages eight and ten, make abstract collages from papers they had painted and having them paint enough extras so I could have some for my own use. We painted papers one morning, and they made their collages the next day, after the paint was dry. They tore their papers and used other designs pulled from magazines. One chose to overlay her design with white tissue. I made my own design after they left for home, when I could think in peace.

This project uses paper that I stamped at home using half an onion, and the papers painted by my granddaughters. My only request to them was that they stay within a limited color range on any one paper. I cut out triangles of different sizes and angles from the assembled papers, using a paper cutter for a crisp edge. The largest pieces were glued first. I distributed the patterns throughout the design. Triangles were placed in various directions. The black spaces between the colored triangles are actually part of the design. They formed additional black triangles as if by magic as I glued the colored papers.

Vacations

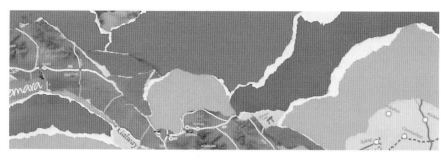

Use maps, photos, and found objects to make a one-page scrapbook to remember a pleasurable trip or vacation. Include local elements, ticket stubs, newspapers, shells and sand from the beach, or pressed flowers and leaves. Part of the fun is in the hunt for objects to recycle.

PROJECT 19. My Ireland

Materials: Torn paper, torn maps—
all found on vacation.
Background: 12 x 16-inch mat board.
Adhesives: Diluted white glue or glue
stick applied to the board and the
torn paper.

I expected Ireland to be green before I saw it. It's known as the Emerald Isle, after all. About one-quarter of the people of the Republic of Ireland live in Dublin, so there seems to be farmland wherever you look throughout the rest of the country. The intensity of the green is overwhelming, deepened by the dark clouds that move swiftly through the sky and the frequent rains that replenish the soil.

I collected all of the papers and maps on a recent vacation, starting with in-flight menus covered in green on Aer Lingus. I also collected green from newspapers and magazines wherever I went. Before I started to glue the collage, I drew the dimensions of the cut mat in light pencil, to act as a guide for the placement of my pieces.

The sky is filled with rain clouds, and the rounded green hills lead down to dark water.

All of the paper is torn, leaving a white deckle edge to separate the pieces from each other. You can practice tearing with a scrap of the same type paper that you'll use in your collage. If you tear one way, the white will appear. Tear in the opposite direction and the white is on the reverse side of the paper.

I tore pieces of green-colored tourist maps in the shape of hills, including some of the place names that I visited. I started gluing from the top and layered pieces working downward on the mat board.

PROJECT 20. North of Santa Fe

Materials: Varied color tissue papers, pressed weeds and grasses, bits of construction paper, textured paper—all found at home or received in trade.

Background: Corrugated cardboard.

Adhesives: Diluted white glue for all the papers, brushed directly to the cardboard. Dots of thick white glue for the pressed grasses.

Time spent in New Mexico is ever imprinted on my mind. The light, the color of the soil, the plants, the sky, the rocks, and the mountains are foreign to my East Coast eyes.

This is one of the simplest designs in the book, but it captures the memories of my last trip. The grasses are some weeds I had picked near home and pressed.

I started with the top of the picture so I could layer until I reached the bottom. Layering gives a feeling of depth to the picture. I tore all of the papers to make the elements seem more natural. I overlapped the various colored tissue papers, using darker colors on the bottom layer and lighter on the top. Note the yellow "sun" to the top right. As I added the papers, I didn't try to get them completely smooth; I wanted to achieve a textured landscape.

PROJECT 21. Art Deco Historic District

Materials: Photos I took of Art Deco architecture, beach sand, cut and torn colored paper.

Background: Foam core, 16 x 20 inches and old photo mat.

Adhesives: At the start of the project I sprayed the mat with Tack 2000, according to directions on the can, let the spray dry for thirty seconds, sprinkled on the dry sand, and pressed down with a gloved hand. I did this spraying outdoors for proper ventilation. After it seemed as if the sand was well and truly stuck, I gave another light spray on the top surface. Photos and other papers attached with glue stick or white glue.

A one-week vacation in winter took my daughter and me to South Florida. We stayed two nights in South Beach, and also two in Homestead, within spittin' distance of the Everglades. A collage or scrapbook page about the trip could take in many themes: alligators and other wildlife, vegetation, restaurants and sightseeing activities, lying on the beach, and so on. I chose here to stick to one theme, the enthralling Art Deco architecture of the historic district, the glamorous design of my childhood. Art Deco design uses machine-inspired forms, symmetry, round porthole windows, and curved edges and corners. Of course palm trees are ubiquitous in that part of the state, and I created them with small cut bits of found colored papers. I imported about a cup of genuine Florida sand directly from the beach in a Ziploc bag. Is that allowed?

I printed out photos in various sizes (3 x 5 and 4 x 6) on plain paper at the highest resolution and cut out any sky and unwanted elements. Then I traced the mat on the board and marked the interior cut size with a pencil.

As I glued the pieces to the board, I went a little outside the line so no background would show in the finished picture. The sky was formed from cut or torn blue papers. I arranged the building images with the smallest ones near the top, so they seemed farthest away. The bottom of the picture has the largest images.

The mat was prepared with sand and cut palm fronds and trunks. I marked the trunk rings with brown colored pencil to make them look "authentic." Some of the palm fronds and trunks have escaped the body of the picture, resting right on the mat.

PROJECT 22. Everglades with Mom

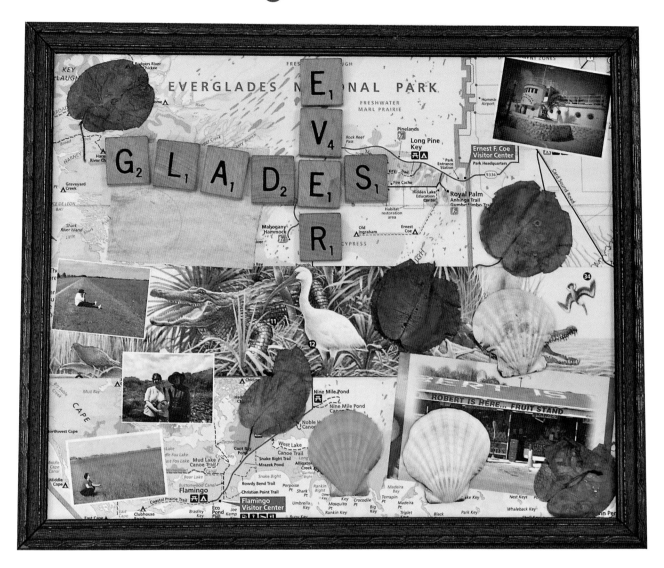

Materials: Map, passport stamp from the Everglades National Park on plain paper, Scrabble tiles from broken set, bougainvillea, shells, photos on plain paper, brochures—all found.

Background: Mat board, 8 x 10 inches. Sand the backs of the wood tiles back before gluing for better adhering

Adhesives: White glue diluted for paper, full strength for tiles and shells.

I asked my daughter, Jen Hopkins, to create a collage of the time we spent together during our South Florida vacation week. I was doing the same. As we collected items for possible use, we tried to hide them from each other and didn't discuss our designs or schemes. In fact, we didn't see each others' collage until we were both finished.

Jen said, "It *was* definitely fun. First, I had a whole stack of papers and things, and narrowed it down to the places we loved, the things that made me smile most about our trip. I was doing this for two days. Then I spent this morning relearning 'less is more' and used only half the things I loved—tossed out the alligator rubber stamps, the Stone Crab matchbook, the Century Hotel lizard. Less really is more; it's just too much to read with too many things. And also it makes the finished work feel like a greatest hits, best-of-show selection of memories of the trip together."

Jen tried to capture highlights of the trip, loosely organized around the red line of the route we took from Homestead to the Flamingo Visitor Center of the Everglades National Park. She glued the map down first.

Hobbies

When a mild interest morphs into a hobby, and a hobby into an obsession, you know you're hooked. Interests evolve over time; what was once an overriding desire to spend time doing an activity is now relegated to a fond memory. I used to love snorkeling, gardening, embroidering, golf, photography, running, biking, canoeing, knitting, and woodworking, among other pursuits. Gather some of the materials and equipment from these former hobbies together and create a collage to remind you of past or present interests.

PROJECT 23. Under Water

Materials: Torn and cut tissue paper, construction paper, honeycomb packing paper, foil-insulated paper bag cut into fish shapes, thin brown corrugated cardboard, silver ribbon, spray paint—all found at home.

Background: Corrugated cardboard, 16 x 20 inches.

Adhesives: Diluted white glue brushed directly on the board for the construction paper and tissue paper. Gel medium (soft gel matte) for the honeycomb packing paper, the bigger fish, and ribbon. Small glue dots for the top layer of honeycomb packing paper (15 dots), the thin brown corrugated cardboard seaweed (2 dots each), the ribbon, and the fish (1 dot each).

There, on top of a cardboard box awaiting the trash man, was a big sheet of crumpled honeycomb paper. The basement of my condo building often offers up such treasures. The paper had obviously been used as part of some packaging but was still pristine. It became the inspiration for this collage.

It's murky and mysterious under water: Fish are hard to see. Seaweed and anemones wave in the current. In order to produce the same feeling I get when snorkeling, I layered the materials, incorporating the painted honeycomb paper to both obscure and allow the viewer to see into the depths.

On layer 1, I brushed glue directly on the board and covered it with the green construction paper, smoothing it out with a plastic card. Then I brushed glue on the board and put down the blue tissue paper.

For layer 2, I brushed the gel medium on the painted green honeycomb paper, which was quite uneven, and pressed it down on the board with a flat hand, allowing layer 1 to peek through. Then I added the fish cut from the insulated paper bag and a piece of braided silver ribbon from my ribbon stash for seaweed.

On layer 3, using the glue dots, I attached the second piece of painted honeycomb paper, allowing the viewer to catch glimpses of the colors and spaces below. Then I added a school of smaller silver fish swimming above the larger school and going in the opposite direction, five short pieces of partially unbraided silver ribbon, and some seaweed torn from the thin wrapper the home-delivery company uses to protect eggs. In case you don't recognize the silver fish, they're cut from the kind of bags supermarkets use to package ice cream. (More ice cream for everyone please!)

I cut the sheet roughly in thirds and grabbed some floral spray paints that had once been sent to me to try: one piece I sprayed Fresh Green; another piece I sprayed with a mix of Hydrangea Blue, Fresh Green, and a little Black Chrome Metallic; and the third piece I sprayed with Terra Rosa and Perfect Pink. When I saw what had happened on the paper, the underwater theme bubbled up. I used the first two painted pieces as layers in this collage, reserving the pinkish one for another time.

PROJECT 24. Printer's Box with Seashells and Fossils

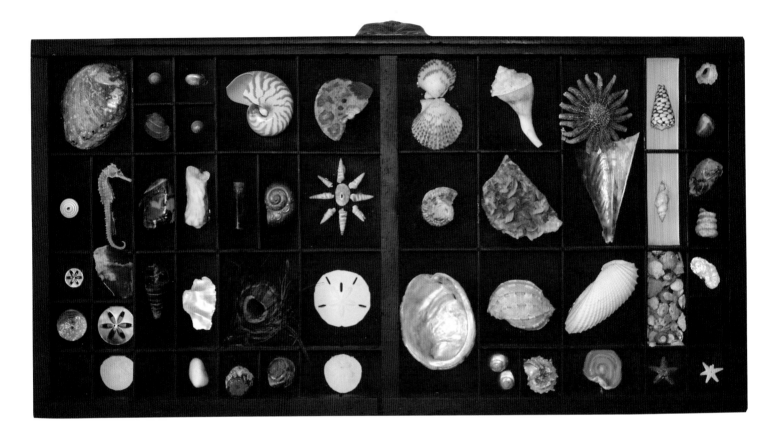

Materials: Ribbon, fossils, shells, sand dollars, buttons, minerals, sand, seahorse, peacock feather—many collected, some purchased.

Background: Old wooden printer's box with original compartments and hardware, painted black.

Adhesives: White glue for light elements. Epoxy glue for heavier elements.

This was my first attempt at serious collage, or assemblage. It hung for fifteen years in our dining room, then in my counseling office, now in my New York studio. The moiré ribbon near the right edge was once a vibrant blue; it's now a mid-gray shade.

A few elements have come loose during various moves and had to be reglued.

The size of the elements pretty much determined which compartments would become their homes. The size of the compartments restricted the size of the elements. As usual, you must find a place for the larger elements first, because there are many choices for the smaller elements, including grouping some together. Except for the ribbon, all elements are their natural colors.

PROJECT 25. The Stuff of Roses

Materials: Old fabrics and lace: gold-wire ribbon, ribbon, feather, lace, doilies—all found at home; and gold and red spray paint, frame.

Background: Clayboard, 16 x 20 inches. I chose this stiff board because I'd be using lots of pieces of fabric that are heavy and there would be no warping. Corrugated cardboard is another option.

Adhesives: White glue for the fabric, brushed directly on the board. The first piece of large fabric should be pulled taut and smooth so the rest of the layers will lie flat. Spray glue for the fabric on the frame.

I admit it. I grow roses. On a rooftop in New York City, I now have them in twelve containers. But the idea for this collage arose when a friend gave me a lovely old piece of fabric and some rose scraps from a Norman Norell blouse of the late 1950s or early '60s. The whole design is built around those three-dimensional roses and the faded beige fabric.

Since I'm using only fabric for this collage, I wanted to use fabric on the frame as well. My daughter found the frame at her town dump. It needed help, so my son-in-law spray-painted it a deep red color.

He also spray-painted some lace with gold. It came on a bolt from the same dump.

I cut the lace in four strips to fit the sides in length, with enough to wrap around to the back of the frame. I mitered the corners of the strips so they met on a slant. Then I sprayed glue directly on the back of one strip of fabric and placed it on the frame and pressed it in place.

I continued spraying and gluing the other three strips, so the final frame looked like this.

The background fabric is cut from a length I bought in Paris fourteen years ago to make a tablecloth. It has been languishing in a drawer awaiting the sewing machine that I gave away long ago. You may have pieces like this stashed away. Collage work is the perfect place to use them. If the fabric has a big print like this, decide before you cut how you want the fabric to run and which part of the print should be centered. Much of it will be obscured in the final design, but as usual it pays to plan ahead.

The rose fabric is a thin silk organdy, but it was triple layered. I cut away the bottom two layers so the pattern and color of my French fabric would show through. I pieced together several scraps of the Norell to make this fan shape as the major form in the piece, yet it too was partially obscured at the end.

I formed roses out of ribbon with wire ties at the bottom to use in this piece, but decided about halfway through to save them for another collage or a special gift wrap. The design process is a constant give and take, adding and subtracting. The doily at the top left is tea-dyed to look old, and cut in half. The doily at bottom left is old and had crocheted pink flowers and green leaves around the border. I cut these off and used them individually at the top right and top left, where the strong color was not overwhelming.

As I started thinking about this piece, I came across a pink feather on the lawn in Central Park and grabbed it. I adore accidental finds of the perfect size and color.

Toward the end of making the collage I wanted a darker piece of fabric on the left to balance some of the heaviness on the right. I started ripping pieces from what I had assembled. The sound of ripping fabric echoes from my childhood where clerks in fabric stores would measure your purchase with a yardstick, take a small snip to start, and then rip the fabric right across the bolt. By some feat of magic, the rip was always straight, the sound as glorious as an ash bat on a baseball for a triple. With my second rip, this purple feather shape appeared, mirroring the found pink feather. I swear it wasn't planned.

PROJECT 26. Eat Your Veggies

Materials: Old seed packets, leftover cilantro seeds, cut paper from magazines, newspapers, and seed catalogs.

Background: Corrugated cardboard, painted with black gesso, 12 x 15 inches.

Adhesives: Soft gel medium (matte) brushed directly on the board. For the seeds, I brushed the gel medium a little thicker and pressed the seeds right into the gel.

Ellen Z., who collects old seed packets, insisted I take her twenty duplicates and "do something with them." Even though they are circa 1910, they didn't look old; they had been printed in chromolithograph and had been packed in boxes until recently. I found making a collage with them to be a real challenge, because the repetition of size and shape is static and boring. I crumpled, pleated, cut, and mauled a few packets, but was still dissatisfied until my daughter Jen made the suggestion of overlaying them with grasses and weeds.

I used nine packets whole and cut the name labels from the other packets. Then I cut small pieces of green, orange, and deep pink papers into long fringes and shaped the tips irregularly. I tore some of the strands out of each fringe, trying to achieve a grassy look. Each pack has one piece of green and one piece of orange or pink covering part of the pack.

Gifts

Something you have made yourself is always appreciated as a gift that comes straight from the heart. While it's true that it may make gift-giving easy on the budget, it's also evident that you put much work and thought into making a collage wall hanging or card.

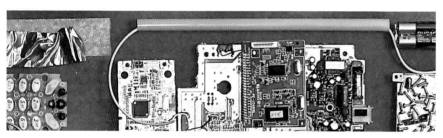

PROJECT 27. This Is My Friend Nana

Materials: Cut paper, felted wool, old silk fabric, sewing thread, beads, gold cord, gold pen, wire, toothpicks—all found at home.

Background: Prestretched canvas, 18 x 14 inches.

Adhesives: Diluted white glue for the papers and sewing thread. Matte medium for the beads, felted wool, fabric, cord. and toothpicks.

Maya, the six-year-old granddaughter of my BFF, admired my cat collage that I sent her via email. Hoping to stimulate her artistic imagination, I described my collage book project and asked Maya for another suggestion. Maya thought I should create a picture of her Nana and me and call it *This Is My Friend Nana.* So here it is. I'm on the left, hips a little slimmer than usual, with a flower bouquet behind me, and Nana is on the right with her glasses and knitting. We are the focal point of the piece, leaning in to each other, arms engaged. We're ready to begin a long conversation as we love to do in a comfy, decorative room.

I placed the rugs and major pieces of furniture first, followed by the lamps and skylight.

Next I placed the torsos, legs, arms, and heads. Last I added the fine details—the hair, facial features, jewelry, and room accessories. I didn't try for accurate facial images, but rather for the overall impression. The woolly top I'm wearing is cut from an old sweater of mine, ready to discard, that I felted in the washer and dryer. Nana, usually dressed more elegant than I, is wearing a top fashioned from scraps of antique silk. I drew frames around the paintings with gold pen.

PROJECT 28. Call Me

Materials: Circuit boards of two discarded hand phones, TV remote control unit, portable CD player and its dismantled screws and parts, CDs, various coated and uncoated wires, batteries, copper garden tags, flower water tubes, two flower stalk holders—all found at home; and one sheet of green textured paper.

Background: Artist's board, complete with wood mounting, 20 x 16 inches. I used the back of the board.

Adhesives: Glue stick for paper. Gel medium for most other parts. Gorilla Glue for the one round speaker, because of its weight. Weigh down any small items as needed to achieve good contact while drying. Wires to hold CDs and plastic tubes.

Trying to escape into the realm of engineering and technology, I started this project by rescuing two handheld phones from the big recycling can in my apartment basement. As a girl, I never investigated the workings of things; I was too busy roaming empty lots in my neighborhood, trying to transplant wild flowers to my garden and attempting to build my own earthworm and silkworm farms.

The industrial look of the Masonite background is not hidden but becomes part of the piece. Electronic items are deconstructed; the parts are treated as design elements rather than having anything to do with their original use. After gluing the small items, I weighed them down as needed to achieve good contact while drying. For tiny bits, like the screws, I painted a coat of gel medium in the small metal tray, and then I dropped in screws, rather than trying to glue each bit individually. Colored wires visually connect various elements. I poked holes in the CDs with a hot skewer and wove coated wires through the holes to attach them. I wove other wires through plastic tubes and through other holes in the components. Copper garden tags were crumpled and used for their color and shine. Flower stalk holders became conduits for wire. Nothing is what it seems.

When I took a small screwdriver in hand to dismantle my electronic treasures, I had no concept of what I would find. The green circuit boards astonished me with their intricacy and strange beauty. It was easy to find two more discarded items shoved to the back of my own shelves. Who will ever again want a portable CD player when all CDs have been downloaded to other devices? I recycled the player into an artwork with the half circle in the upper left corner and round piece on the right side in the middle as the major components. I thank Robert Janvrin, a then twelve-year-old visiting from New Hampshire, for help in the actual design of the assembled pieces.

PROJECT 29. Skezas Grocery

Materials: Original lists, licenses, keys, ads, ephemera from the store, photos, keychain with picture of Mount Rushmore, bottle caps, old package, corrugated cardboard, map of South Dakota—all found at home.

Background: Masonite hardboard with wood surround, 16 x 20 inches.

Adhesives: Soft gel medium for all items.

In 1926, two Greek immigrant brothers founded Skezas Grocery at 504 Third Street in Huron, South Dakota. It was built of brick by Christ Skezas and operated by various family members until 1983. The two brothers and their families originally lived in apartments over the store, but eventually moved out to homes of their own—a familiar story.

During the Depression and after, the Skezases sent boxes of clothing back to relatives in their native village and kept detailed, handwritten lists of what they sent. The store is long gone, and now my relatives-by-marriage, Nick and Yota Karras (Yota is the daughter of one of the original owners; she and her husband were the second generation to run the store), are moving from their home in Huron to a much smaller space near their daughter. What to dump and what to save? This collage is a one-page scrapbook that features artifacts from the store or objects related to it. It will go from my studio in New York City to the Karrases to hang on the wall of their new residence.

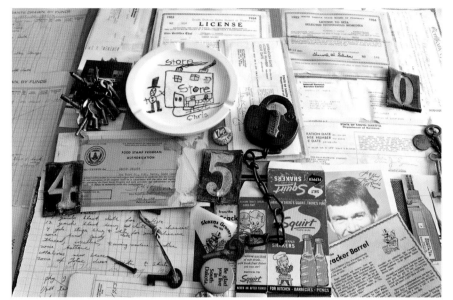

Collage is all about editing. There were many lists of the items sent to Greece; I chose the earliest from 1949. I made other selections from the store's ads and licenses based on the color and sometimes the age. Two items sent to me for the collage I deemed too heavy: an ashtray made by the first-grade son of the store owners in 1963 and a padlock, chain, and key from the Chicago North Western Railroad, where the Skezas brothers delivered groceries in their Ford Model T. I took photos of each and cut them out to incorporate in the design.

The map of South Dakota is recent, from my closet, so to make it look more worn, I smeared it with used espresso grounds and wiped off the excess with a paper towel. While the map was still damp from its coffee facial, I crumpled it in my hands and then straightened it out and let it dry. With this treatment it seems to fit in better with the other artifacts. The Karrases also sent me a huge ring of keys from the store; I used most of them around the edges to enhance the frame.

The address numbers 504 had been removed from the shop. I placed them in a position of prominence, partially framing the name "Huron" on the map. To make them stand out even more, I cut small rectangles out of corrugated cardboard, glued them to the map, and then glued the numerals to the cardboard. This technique produces small shadows around the edges.

PROJECT 30. Grandma Roses

Materials: Old rose botanical print, ad for rose nursery, copies of Redouté rose prints, pressed roses and rose leaves, torn calligraphy, paper with bamboo leaves—all found at home, and old fabric roses from a trade, watercolor paints.

Background: Corrugated cardboard, 25 x 12 inches.

Adhesives: Diluted white glue.

This piece makes a nice gift for a gardener or anyone who loves roses. Some of the elements are nearly one hundred years old. Some, like the fabric roses, are about fifty years old. Other elements were treated to seem antique.

First, I measured and cut the bamboo paper to cover the corrugated board.

On my home copier, I reproduced the Redouté rose drawings that were on manufactured notecards. This way I am able to use the copies for the collage and still retain the cards for future use. I tore the main images to a manageable size.

Since I wanted the whole piece to look old, I tea-dyed all the papers that had a pure white background, including the cut-out words "Beyond the Garden," the subtitle of an earlier book I wrote called *Easy and Elegant Rose Designs.*. I painted the fabric roses and some paper roses with pale pink watercolor. I made a plan and laid out all the elements, moving them around until I had a pleasing layout. I glued on the biggest elements first, followed by the smaller elements. There's lots of layering is going on here.

PROJECT 31. Easy as ABC

Materials: Cut paper graphics—all found at home or printed on home computer.

Background: Ready-made shadowbox frames, 8 x 12 inches, with mats that hold 4-x-6 photos.

Adhesives: Glue stick for each letter. I didn't want this mat to warp with too much wet glue as it would have been hard to weigh down to straighten.

This gift is for a new baby, but the idea could work as easily for an adult. Just change ABC to your friend's initials. My initials, ESP, work perfectly. Use letters in a short nickname or a secret code. Do you need to remind someone to mind their Ps and Qs? Use two frames. Or to work PDQ? QED. I rest my case.

Design Tips & Techniques: For this size frame, I used 288-point Engravers MT font for the biggest A, B, and C. I also printed out a few smaller letters using red ink on white paper and blue ink on green paper. As this is a baby gift, I stuck to all capital letters, no lowercase or script. For an older child or adult, you could take much more leeway with the fonts and still be understood.

I sorted all of the letters into three piles—small, medium, and large—and then tried them around the frame to make sure I had enough to almost cover the mat. I glued the largest letters first, then the medium ones, and then the small ones, tilting some and overlapping, trying to make each letter readable. I saved four of the smallest of each of the letters to glue to the corners of the wood frames. The collages have three levels of letters for even greater depth.

Holidays

Halloween is the time for masks. A collage mask is sure to please. A small collage can also double as a greeting card; write a personal message on the front or back. It will surely be prized above any mass-produced cards, but will cost little in time or money. Design cards for Christmas, Halloween, Mother's Day, Get Well, Graduation, New Year's, or simply to say You're My Friend. Make it on a stiff-paper background or on a small piece of corrugated cardboard, but make sure it can stand. Personalize your card for the recipient and it is likely to be saved among that person's treasures.

PROJECT 32. The Mask

Materials: Corrugated cardboard, mat board, honeycomb packing paper.

Background: Corrugated cardboard cut to shape with the sharp blade of a craft knife, here 17 x 21 inches.

Adhesives: Gel medium for all flat pieces of corrugated cardboard. Glue gun and glue sticks for hair and pieces that must stand on edge. For each curl of hair, use one glue dot, either at an end or in the middle to let both ends curl.

A mask to hide behind? Hang on your wall? Scare people at Halloween? Whatever you decide, the mask is fun to make.

The art is in transforming flat materials into a three-dimensional collage full of angles and shadows. Use the same techniques for any abstract, human, or animal form created from a readily available discard—a corrugated carton.

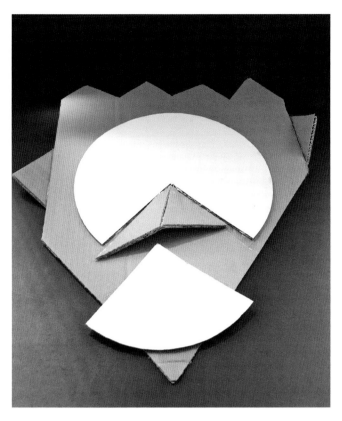

Although the materials were originally flat, I've created a three-dimensional mask by layering, bending, and curling layers of corrugated cardboard and mat board. You can practice cutting corrugated board using some extra pieces cut from a carton. Also practice ripping off layers from the board and exploring the various textures that appear. Use a cutting mat underneath to protect your table.

Here, I scored pieces of cardboard lightly and then bent them to make the ears and nose. I tried for an approximation of a human face, with a pointed chin and spiked hair. I rescued the big white circle from underneath a bakery cake, wiped it off, and then cut out a wedge to use in the mouth area. I found some cardboard with precut circles and one piece with precut rectangles and incorporated them into the design of the eyes and mouth. I wanted to keep this piece all neutral, using only white and tan paper and board. You could paint or use oil pastel to color any sections you wanted.

I peeled very thin layers for the hair curls. I used scraps of cream mat board and peeled off layers for additional curls. If a scrap didn't want to curl, I rolled it in a coil and then unrolled it, and a curl appeared by magic. The eyebrows are cut from a piece of honeycomb packaging paper. To hang, affix an adhesive hanger to the back.

I added wire ringlets to the hairstyle by first coiling one-foot lengths of thin copper wire around a pen, then sliding them off and stretching them out slightly. I poked one end of the wire all the way through the background and bent it down on the reverse side to adhere to the mask.

The Mask: Part *Deux*

All neutral, indeed! My bead collection beckoned to me and so did some copper wire. Before I knew it I had a different, sadder mask.

My jar contained one tear-shaped bead, and it was obvious where that should go. The other glitter came from a bracelet I found one morning as I was tending the tree plots in front of my apartment building in New York City. No one was around to claim it—a gift from the collage gods, no doubt. The bracelet was easy to cut into pieces without losing the backing with its beads. All beads were glued in place with soft gel medium.

PROJECT **33.** It Was a Very Good Year

Materials: Wine corks, pieces of grapevine, red and white candle stubs, cut and torn paper, silver wire—all found at home; and gold pen, tissue paper, watercolor paints.

Background: Sheet of Bristol Board, 11 x 14 inches, folded.

Adhesives: Red candle drippings for wine corks, metal coil, and pieces of grapevine. White glue or permanent glue stick for the papers.

To celebrate the New Year or any festive occasion, or for friends who are wine aficionados, make a small collage like this that can serve as a greeting card. Fold a sheet of Bristol board or heavy paper before you start so you'll know the space in which you'll work. In your best script, add a greeting inside: "You Pop My Cork!" or something more clever and personal. You may not want to send this card through the mail, however, lest it gets squished.

To make the metal coil for the flower stem, I cut a length of wire about three times longer than I wanted for the finished piece. Then I wrapped the wire tightly around a fat pen. After slipping the spiral off the pen, I stretched the wire out slightly, making the coil to the length I wanted. To fasten the coil, wine corks, and grapevine, I lit the red candle, held it carefully upside down, and let the wax drip where I wanted it. I worked on one section at a time, letting the wax solidify before working on the next section.

For the wax round in the upper right, I dripped a quantity of white candle wax on the paper. When it was almost hard, I pressed in the bottom of a small kitchen eggbeater to give the wax texture. I then added a few drops of red candle wax in the middle. I layered the yellow tissue paper over the picture of the wine glass to make that image more subtle. Then I tinted areas of the background with diluted red watercolor paint.

PROJECT 34. Will You Be Mine?

Materials: Old fabrics, cut and torn newspaper and magazine papers, painted paper, canceled U.S. stamp—all found at home.

Background: Precut corrugated cardboard, 8 inches diameter. The stand is 9 x 2¼ inches, cut from another piece of corrugated cardboard.

Adhesives: Staples to attach the cardboard stand to the back of the round. Soft gel matte medium for the fabric and papers.

Greeting cards come in all shapes and sizes when you make them yourself. This one began with the round cardboard support under a small lemon tart from the bakery. Usually I make my own tarts, but I bought this as a special treat. The cardboard was a bonus, because I have a hard time cutting a perfect circle with a craft knife. When I wiped off this round to save with my collage supplies, I had no idea of its final destination. Searching for a Valentine card background, it was perfect.

Because the attached cardboard stand folds flat, this card could be mailed easily. The used LOVE stamp dates back to when first-class mail in the U.S. was less than half of what it is now. Ink lines run through the stamp as part of the cancellation process. Beware that your sweetie doesn't infer that your love has been canceled.

I'm hoping the recipient will want to save this card, even display it on his desk, so I designed a stand and attached it to the back as the first order of business. I copied the cardboard stand from a purchased desk frame that I own. I bent down the top inch and stapled it to the round.

Next, I cut the fabric so there would be enough to drape over the edge and glue to the back. Here I patched together pieces of two different fabrics. The fabric hides the staples. When gluing down the fabric, I brushed the gel medium on the cardboard, smoothing on the front and pulling gently to attach it on the back. I started with more materials than I needed. This is a small collage, so I used only two big hearts and glued them down first.

All the other pieces were layered on top. The curve of one heart sneaks out over the rim of the background. If you're meticulous, you can "wallpaper" the back with plain or fancy paper to hide the fabric edges. Write a personal message on the back or on one of the hearts in front.

Abstract

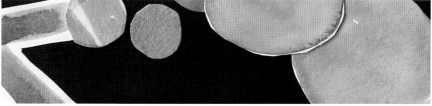

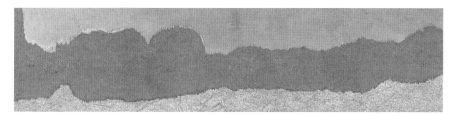

In making an abstract collage, the artist begins with no concrete object or theme in mind. She or he may use irregular areas of color to express spontaneous impressions without representing any particular thing. Or an abstract could show a quality, emotion, or general idea of a thing. It's also true that the viewer may perceive an object not intended by the artist, as happens in a Rorschach inkblot test.

PROJECT 35. Tree Track

Materials: Newspaper, white tissue paper, colored sparkles—all found at home; and acrylic paint.

Background: Sheet of drawing paper, 11 x 16 inches.

Adhesives: Golden soft gel brushed on the back of painted tissue and newspaper. Glitter sprinkled on the surface of the paper in places where soft gel appears.

Judith Wolfson created *Tree Track* in a class on abstract collage and mixed media at the Art Center of Sarasota. She likes to work with abstractions, which she says gives her an open forum to use any materials and create any effects. Judith, a Philadelphian in summer, made this piece in February in the Florida warmth, but was thinking of the winter up north and the slush and tracks cars make in the snow.

Judith brushed a thin application of Golden Polymer matte finish on the drawing paper for texture. She tore newspaper and white tissue in pieces and brushed one side of the pieces with acrylic paints in blue, red, or black. Some pieces tore during the painting process, but that was part of the textural effect that she was seeking.

When the paint dried, she brushed soft gel on the back of the paper and rolled it onto the background with a brayer, and more tearing and ripping ensued. She suggests that if you don't have a brayer, a cardboard roll from toilet paper works just fine when you don't need to apply a lot of pressure.

Judith glued the trunk of the tree down first, then the other pieces. She made the tracks of paint on the background paper by dipping the edge of an old credit card in acrylic paint and running it over the white background surface. She suggests that if you blow-dry the work with a hair dryer, you can create even more texture, because some areas dry faster than others.

PROJECT 36. Exuberance

Materials: Cut and torn pieces of watercolor drawings.
Background: Black end sheet from a pad of watercolor paper on white cardboard, 16 x 13 inches.
Adhesives: All papers glued on with rubber cement.

Judith Benson, currently a student at the Art Students League in New York City, created her collage *Exuberance* from torn and cut pieces of earlier watercolor drawings. As a warm-up for each class, Judith's teacher asks students to make a black watercolor sketch of one-minute poses of a live model. In one minute, the student must avoid detail and disregard color, but capture the essence of movement in the figure.

Judith tore six warm-up sketches from larger pieces of her past papers and arranged them to keep the movement flowing throughout the collage. She added colorful pieces from other "failed" watercolors and made them look like playthings. Notice that the figure at the bottom left holds a ball cut from the piece at the bottom right. In this collage, Judith is interested in the negative space; she says that all of the black in the background is as important as the figures in the foreground.

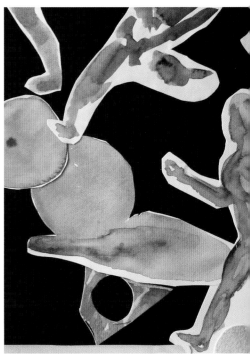

PROJECT 37. Big Sky Country

Materials: Ribbon, torn pictures of sky and blue papers from newspapers, magazines, and old calendars—all found at home; and one piece of purchased textured paper.

Background: Corrugated cardboard, 14¹/₄ x 11¹/₂ inches.

Adhesives: Diluted white glue or glue stick for all papers. Diluted white glue for the ribbon.

In the beginning I wanted to create an abstract of sky. I gathered pieces of blue paper and a ribbon and then designed, glued, and examined the finished project. Low and behold, mountains and a stream had appeared without my knowing it. Start with one idea and the final project may morph into another. Everyone who's viewed this picture also sees mountains and water, so those features must be *there* in my abstract. Accept the inevitable.

 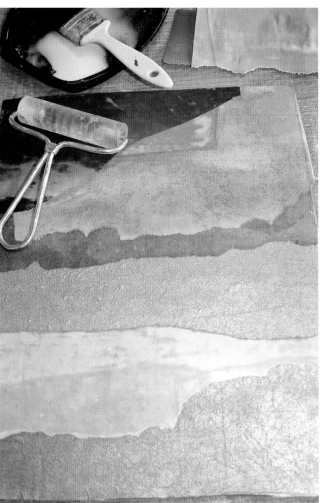

I tore all the paper edges rather than cut them, to achieve a wispy look. After arranging the papers, I walked away. I then came back several times to look, trying papers in different positions, layering them.

When I was ready, I glued on the bottom layer, rolling out the air bubbles with a brayer, and then added papers, working my way to the surface.

PROJECT 38. Big Sky Country with Umbrella

Materials: Three copies of one photo, cotton from pill bottle, seed beads, ribbon, cocktail umbrella—all found at home.

Background: Cardboard, 11 x 14 inches.

Adhesives: Diluted white glue for paper. Full-strength white glue for ribbon, cotton, beads, and cocktail umbrella.

When I photograph a landscape, I focus on the mountains, trees, or buildings as the objects of interest; the sky is secondary. Here, the sky is the main image, and the repetition gives it added strength.

I printed out three copies of one image that includes lots of sky and then cut off any white borders and parts of the landscape, so that only the sky remained. I glued these down one over the other and slightly over-lapping, starting from the bottom, smoothing out air bubbles with a brayer or plastic card before going on to the next piece. The cotton on top of some of the cloud images was added for texture. I brushed the full-strength white glue directly on the image surface to add the ribbon, beads, and umbrella, carefully press-ing down on the items to attach them.

PROJECT 39. Bursting

Materials: Torn and cut paper, tissue paper, pressed ginkgo leaves—all found at home; and blue iridescent paper, repurposed painted paper.
Background: Bristol board, 11 x 14 inches.
Adhesives: Glue stick for papers. Dabs of Tacky Glue for the leaves.

Color and movement define this abstract, but try as I may I can't seem to get away from an appearance of sky and leaves falling. What do you see?

All of the materials in this collage are lightweight, so the Bristol board is a fine background. I wanted the white edges of the torn paper to show. If I didn't, I would tear from the other direction. Experiment with tearing before you start with your best pieces and you'll see how the edges differ depending on the direction of the tear. I glued down the biggest pieces first. Aqua tissue paper overlaps some of these. Here the starburst and the ginkgo leaves form the topmost layer. I pressed the leaves in fall when they were this rich gold color.

Seasons of the Year

With each new season I have renewed energy for the pleasures it will bring. Spring means anticipating green growth, gardening, outdoor tennis, and the scent of rain. Summer brings the warmth of the sun, picnics, a walk in the park, the beach, swimming, amusement parks, and baseball. Fall, of course, is about the colors of the leaves, crisp night air, pumpkin harvest, the sun lower on the horizon, the last of the asters, and learning something new, just as in those many years of schooling. And winter means skiing, visiting friends in warm climates, holiday decorations, and fresh snow. As each season starts I want to design a collage that expresses my feelings.

PROJECT 40. Summer Water Lilies

Materials: Painted paper, one photo image printed out in two sizes, copper wire in two sizes, piece of green translucent envelope—all found at home; and gold crinkled paper, thin brass nails.

Background: Pale green mat board on foam core, 16 x 16 inches.

Adhesives: Glue stick for the papers. The gold tacks pierce the translucent envelope, attaching it to the background. Copper wire winds around the tacks in random fashion.

The water lily pond at Longwood Gardens outside Philadelphia is a glorious sight in summer, nestled behind the grand conservatory. On one of my many visits, several of the giant leaves had been removed by a gardener and were lying reverse-side up on the concrete surrounding the pond. I grabbed my ever-present camera and captured this sight that normally only the frogs get to see. Until then I never knew that the color and texture of the underside were so interesting.

I printed out the image in 8 x 10 and cut off the white borders. Next, I printed out the same image in 6 x 8, cutting and discarding everything in the image beyond the main stem. I lined up the stems to form a reverse S shape. Then I cut out one floating lily pad from another image. I begged a whole sheet of painted paper from my ten-year-old granddaughter, because it shimmered in a lily pond way.

Pieces cut from a green translucent envelope add to the watery feel. I left the original circle from the envelope, because the shape mimics the curves of the stem. The copper wire ties it all together.

PROJECT 41. Autumn Skyline, West Side

Materials: Cut photos, yellow net bag for onions, torn newsprint, gold paper—all found at home; and strong tea mixture for dying.
Background: Mat board, 20 x 16 inches.
Adhesives: Diluted white glue or glue stick.

As the seasons change, even the city wears different colors. As I peer down on roof gardens in autumn, I'm impressed with the gold and russet trees. In this collage, I decide to add more trees and shrubs to the New York skyline. What power!

I printed out four different images of the autumn skyline on plain paper and cut away the sky from all of the photos. Torn newsprint is perfect for my plan of a sky of yellow hues. Torn clouds are made from papers, and a piece of a yellow net bag is added for texture. I placed the farthest buildings just beneath the sky level, overlapping slightly, cutting the photos so they'll fit. Buildings are from photos and cut bits of paper. I placed them in layers, until I reached the bottom of the picture. For accent, I added small pieces of gold paper and a few torn images of trees and shrubs to green the rooftops. One large roof dormer on the right was too blue, so I washed over it with a strong tea solution, giving it an antique look.

PROJECT 42. The Garden in Winter

Materials: Cut paper from store shopping bags, cut-out magazine pictures, cut construction paper, pressed lavender leaves—all found at home; and one sheet of brown textured paper.

Background: Textured clayboard, 11 x 14 inches, rigid so it will not warp.

Adhesives: Soft gel medium (matte).

I used just four hues: gray, green, brown, and orange. There are five tones of green, two of gray, two of brown, and one of orange. Even though I had cut up some light blue tiles for sky and some other tones of gray and green, I didn't use them in the final project. I also cut and rejected some small white bits I had cut to sprinkle on as snow. Always start with more than you think you'll need so you'll have choices as you work. First cut the papers in long strips about ¹/₂ inch wide, then into tiles. When I started I wanted them all to be the same size but soon found that would be way more trouble than I cared to take. The fact that the tiles are all slightly different in no way detracts from the scene (I claim).

On a freezing day in January, I headed to the Brooklyn Botanic Garden for a meeting of horticultural professionals. My trusty Canon camera was swinging from my shoulder, though this was not a photographic expedition. The sight I glimpsed at the Japanese Hill-and-Pond Garden is etched in my mind even without a digital image—an almost white sky, dark evergreens, a frozen pond with a dusting of snow, and emerging from the frozen water, a bright orange torii gate, symbol of the Shinto religion. Here it is, formed of small paper mosaic tiles.

This was an experiment in mosaic tile work, in which I cut papers with a home paper cutter and scissors into small rectangular or square tiles. Small units are pasted individually to form the picture as a whole. The scene at the garden had much more detail: dead reeds in the water, low-growing bare trees on the hill, more

color variation in the ice, and a strip of black across the torii gate. I stripped the image down to its bare essentials: ice, evergreens, sky, a small fence bordering the pond, a grassy slope, and a few grasses in the foreground.

The textured white of the clayboard background forms the sky, making the background an element in the collage. I started with the ice on the bottom, brushing the gel medium directly on the board and then laying down the tiles.

For the next layers, I brushed the gel medium directly on each tile and put each one down with tweezers. I worked my way up from the fence to the grassy slope and the trees.

The torii was the last part of the image. I placed it off-center, just the way I composed my original photo. After looking at the finished collage for a week, I added a few gray leaves in the foreground.

Notice that the trees are different sizes, the way they are in nature. Also, I had drawn the trunk of the tree, but later decided to cover it with more dark tiles.

PROJECT 43. Spring Has Sprung

Materials: Cut and torn paper, hand-painted paper, brown craft paper, tissue paper, piece of embroidered ribbon that had unraveled, coriander seeds—all found at home.
Background: Mat board on foam core, 16 x 16 inches.
Adhesives: Soft gel medium (matte).

A gold burst of forsythia bushes announces that it's spring at last. Cherry trees and crabapples celebrate in pink. I'm ready to forget winter. I adapt the traditional Tree of Life form into a spring festival. This same tree, with fewer mosaic pieces, could be turned into a family tree or a display of family pets.

On a piece of brown craft paper I drew one side of the tree, with many branches and twigs. The trunk is thicker at the bottom and gets narrower as it reaches the top. The ends of the limbs and twigs are also narrower than the part that attaches to the trunk. I then folded the paper loosely in half the long way and carefully cut out both sides of the tree simultaneously. You may want a large scissors for the bigger areas and a smaller scissors for the intricate parts.

I unfolded the tree and glued down the trunk only, leaving the limbs loose. Next, I cut out strips of colored paper and then cut the strips in squares of different sizes. The largest here is one inch, the smallest $1/4$ inch. I used three main colors to represent spring: green, yellow, and pink. Some of the paper I painted by hand before cutting, so it would appear textured, not flat. I glued the colored squares individually, using a small brush. I first placed some squares under the limbs, letting them peek out from the branches and twigs. After gluing down the tree limbs, I added many more cut squares on the trunk and branches. The roots are an important part of this design; they are made from embroidered ribbon that came from my mother's old sewing box and had started to unravel. I picked the threads a little more so the roots would be longer and spread them out, putting glue on the mat board and pressing the threads down to attach them. At the end of the design I wanted even more texture so I spread glue on the trunk and added a layer of coriander seeds. Finally, I rolled pink tissue paper into little balls and added them to the ends of the twigs. Notice on the partially completed picture the trunk and large limbs have some additional coloring rubbed on with a brown crayon. I decided this wasn't needed and covered it all up with the squares.

Because I Wanted To

Inspiration can come from anywhere. Often, it's the found stuff that makes me create.

PROJECT 44. Time on My Hands

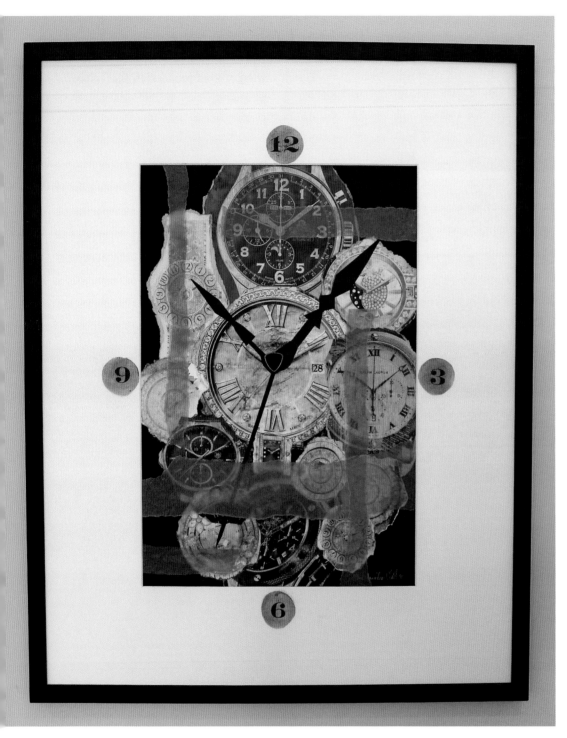

Materials: Torn and cut paper, used espresso grounds, parchment paper, construction paper, part of an earring, sandpaper, pencil, bottle cap—all found at home.

Background: Black foam core, enclosed in cut mat and frame, 23 x 29 inches.

Adhesives: Glue stick for all papers. Gel matte medium for the earring piece, because it's heavy.

The newspaper came with a huge color insert advertising an upcoming watch fair in New York. The pictures were large, luscious, and arresting. What's a girl to do except use them in a clock collage?

Next, I glued the watch images to the black foam core. Then I drew clock hands on black construction paper and cut them out with a small scissors; I pasted a piece of an earring, whose mate had been lost, to the fulcrum of the hands. Finally, I tore five strips of regular kitchen parchment paper in different widths and lengths and pasted the strips on top of the watches to render parts of the picture less bold.

I tore many images of watches from a newspaper insert. To make them look old, I rubbed each with some used, damp espresso grounds and then wiped off the excess with a paper towel. I erased most of the brand names by rubbing with fine sandpaper. I gently ironed on the reverse side any papers that rippled, getting them flat enough for my taste.

On my home printer I printed numbers in a favorite font, here Engravers MT at 72 points, using honey-colored construction paper. I traced circles around the numbers with a small bottle lid. Before cutting them out, I treated the numbers with the same espresso-ground rub as the watch pictures. I then glued these on the four sides of the mat that encloses the collage.

PROJECT 45. The Weaver

Materials: Torn and cut papers, purple pressed leaves, bamboo skewers, wax strips—all found at home; and one piece of purchased fig bark paper, spray paint.

Background: Stretched canvas on wood frame, 9 x 12 inches.

Adhesives: Staples to attach warp paper strips to the back of the wood frame. Soft gel medium to attach all other elements.

It all started on an airplane. Aer Lingus offered small skewers of grilled chicken to accompany drinks. A tasty appetizer, but the best part was the size and shape of the bamboo skewers that held the chicken. I had three, but knew I needed more for a collage: a fan, rowboat oars, picket fence? I pictured myself walking up and down the aisles of business class asking other travelers if I could have their used skewers, but rejected that idea. Instead, I confessed to a friendly flight attendant that I needed many for an art project and she gladly produced a plastic bag with all she collected when she removed the trays. Brought home and scrubbed in soapy water, they're perfect in a weaving.

I spray painted the canvas front and four sides in gold with an overlay of black metal; I had them both on my shelf, but could have used gesso or acrylic instead. While the canvas dried, I tore six strips of peach paper along the edge of a ruler. Handmade papers like this will produce a rough edge when torn. I placed a strip on the canvas, wrapped it around the sides, and stapled it to the back at top and bottom, but not too tightly. I left a slight bit of wiggle room for weaving. Notice that I haven't glued the strips yet, because I want to be able to weave weft strips under and over the warp.

Add the other strips with uneven space between them. I cut additional strips using gold paper from chocolate bars, sponge-painted construction paper made at home, purple paper from a magazine, and a newspaper that received spray paint when I was protecting a surface while making other projects. See, *nothing* gets thrown away. Notice that the strips vary in width and length. I painted glue on the back of a weft strip and carefully wove it across the peach warp, then kept weaving and gluing down the canvas.

Next, I glued on the bamboo skewers and added more vertical strips on top of everything.

Then I added other horizontal strips where there was room and purple leaves that I had pressed (flowering plum and black cotton) as a color accent. Short strips of purple wax saved from an aged gouda cheese and cut with a paring knife add additional color and texture. With a skewer, I placed dabs of glue under any strips that looked loose and pressed down. The result looks like everything is woven in, but some layers are just glued on top of others.

PROJECT 46. Bird Box

Materials: Handcrafted tin birds made by women from a co-op in Oaxaca, Mexico, felt birds by others, twigs pruned from a crimson-bark Japanese maple in my garden, cinnamon sticks saved from a long-forgotten Christmas wreath, purple cardboard box from chocolates presented by a dinner guest, 3-inch wreath, spun silver from my Christmas box, yellow paper from a CD, U.S. postage stamp.

Background: Wooden box, 11 x 15 inches. The box is constructed with open spaces on all four sides.

Adhesives: Small pieces of twisted copper wire to secure branches and cinnamon. One carpet tack suspends the big bird. Soft gel medium for all other elements.

A box found atop the piles of black garbage bags on trash day! My daughter-in-law Linda P. knew it was a treasure and could be reused when she saw it curbside during her morning walk. Here it's the perfect home for some birds I've collected over the years that were stored away deep in a closet.

Sometimes a box can completely enclose the elements displayed within. Remember *Grandma's Sewing Box* on page 28. Here I am literally thinking outside the box. The birds want to fly free. Twigs grow wildly through three sides. I have too much stuff to contain it all in this small box. Even so must I edit carefully and leave most of my birds for other collages. With most collages you are working in two dimensions, even as you build up layers. Here you start with three dimensions and must plan how to use the depth.

I glued on the purple box in the lower left to serve as a platform for the orange bird and to move the small red bird forward. The big red bird hangs from the exterior. Twigs grow through slats of the box into the third dimension. I use the box top as a shelf for other materials. Visually, the size of the box expands by about one-third. With a box that you'll eventually hang, it's very important to keep checking the design while it's upright. Hammer the hanging mechanism on the back before you've added too much to the front; that way you won't damage your work when you invert it.